# Editing
# While Black

### a memoir

**SHANA N. MURPH**

# Editing
# While
# Black

*a memoir*

SHANA N. MURPH

REVISE AND REWRITE EDITORIAL
PHILADELPHIA

Copyright © 2024 Shana N. Murph

All rights reserved. No part of this book may be reproduced in any form or by any electronic or mechanical means, including information storage and retrieval systems, without permission in writing from the publisher, except by reviewers, who may quote brief passages in a review.

ISBN: 978-1-7361985-6-8 (paperback)
ISBN: 978-1-7361985-5-1 (e-book EPUB)
ISBN: 978-1-7361985-4-4 (hardcover)

Library of Congress Control Number: 2023951722

Design by DTPerfect Book Design

www.reviseandrewrite.com
Printed in the United States of America
Published by Revise and Rewrite Editorial, LLC

# CONTENTS

**INTRODUCTION**
The Scarcity of Black Book Editors   *1*

**CHAPTER 1**
Ink to Paper   *9*

**CHAPTER 2**
Nittany Lions and Literary Giants   *29*

**CHAPTER 3**
Conforming to Style   *45*

**CHAPTER 4**
Form and Fashion   *59*

**CHAPTER 5**
Commas and Conjunctions   *71*

**CHAPTER 6**
Shift P   *95*

**CHAPTER 7**
Colorado Take Two   *105*

## CHAPTER 8
Return, New Paragraph   *123*

## CHAPTER 9
Colon   *141*

## CHAPTER 10
Dash   *157*

## CHAPTER 11
Reflections   *177*

## Introduction

# THE SCARCITY OF BLACK BOOK EDITORS

In the 1830s abolitionist David Ruggles opened America's first Black-owned bookstore in the Tribeca section of New York. As an operator for the Underground Railroad, he hid many enslaved African Americans as they journeyed to freedom, including Frederick Douglass. To further the mission to end slavery, he self-published pamphlets and published the first journal edited by an African American, *The Mirror of Liberty*. Although a remarkable human being, hero and pioneer, I never heard his story growing up. I didn't hear much about African American involvement in book publishing or editing. Black people have published their works using their own printing presses for centuries. These facts aren't spoken of enough and their stories are often buried.

When I started editing more than 20 years ago, Black book editors were not a huge part of the book-editing world and in 2023, only 3.5% of book editors were Black. In fact, the only Black book editor I'd ever heard of was the late Toni Morrison who worked at Random House before she transitioned into becoming an author. It seemed like editing was something white people did. At the helm of book publishing were white women—some feminists, some allies, some opportunists, and some elites. Black people in my community were creators, art visionaries, trendsetters, idea generators, inventors, institution owners and movement originators. Black people thrived in the realm of creativity and ingenuity. We were often responsible for lifting humanity as we rose—up from oppression and socio-economic control. We battled for control over our own creative selves and the masterpieces we created. Editors were like the rein holders and the shot callers of the creative world. They controlled what was published and how it was presented. When I read novels, short stories, poetry and other books written by Black authors, I realized, most of the time, these works were printed by publishing houses staffed and led by white editors.

At every company I was always the only Black book editor. Usually, white women were the authority over all titles, which included controlling the reach and presentation of Black voices and other voices of color. On the rare occasions I would hear about Black editors, they were often the sole editors in those companies. They were alone, and their level of influence was limited. This was in the early 2000s. "Publishing so white" was a statement riddled with exclamation points back then. White editors were capable, gracious, deserving and permanently situated as the gatekeepers. It was such a loud and emphatic message. There was almost no room for me. Historically, white men dominated and led printing and publishing companies. These companies had access to Black narratives, Black stories, and if they wanted, they could even limit the exposure Black experiences received.

Control over content has always been just as important as control over the human body, which is why book publishers have always maintained a white power structure—from publisher all the way down to editorial assistant. That is changing somewhat at a few major commercial presses, but there is still a sense of entitlement—an attitude about what Black people

## THE SCARCITY OF BLACK BOOK EDITORS

possess and create. Controlling written materials like books, letters, essays, reports and research helps to solidify whose story gets cemented in time as history. Oppression of content is just as pervasive, destructive and dangerous as the oppression of the physical body. Where physical oppression restricts the freedoms of Black people—preventing them from access, voting and due process—oppression through the written word controls mindsets. Whoever controls the mind has a much easier time restricting and progressing other forms of oppression. Written information impacts laws, establishes reputations, shapes the public's views and inspires action. So, of course, controlling written words can lead to increased power.

Publishing has been the more silent force behind controlling what the public reads and learns. So, when I entered the publishing field, I was never given complete autonomy regarding how Black history, Black voices and Black experiences were presented. Older staff who had been involved in publishing Black authors for decades overshadowed me. I often worked with white authors, which was like a mixed bag of apples, delicious red and tart green—attitudes of every type, sweet and easy, complex and human. Whenever books centered on Black experiences came through the pipeline, I wasn't necessarily a part of the process. Being Black didn't mean every book with Black content or a Black author was assigned to me. What was problematic was that there wasn't necessarily a qualified editor on staff to understand unfamiliar perspectives.

Virtually all vice presidents and CEOs were also white. Black editors could influence but rarely did they take the reins completely. Throughout my corporate career I spent a lot of time being overly nice and unintentionally smart. Sometimes I could speak freely as an employee and even bring about change, but I didn't have complete authority to implement policy or procedure. Complete control requires ownership. Honestly, thinking about it now, it wasn't ownership that was most attractive; it was liberty. In a more literal sense, the quest for freedom was at the forefront of many early writers and publishers. David Ruggles, and others like R.H. Boyd, Ida B. Wells-Barnett, Marcus Garvey, the Murray brothers, Rebecca Lee Crumpler and Susie Taylor, published their works to express and usher in freedom—freedom to think and write for oneself, tell the story or provide expertise. We've always had to insert ourselves into every conversation and movement.

Black-owned publishers of the '60s inserted themselves into the industry, publishing the works of Black authors. They had not penetrated the market like many major publishers, but Black publishers thrived in the Black community. Even more so, journalism became Black people's main avenue for publishing and distributing content to the mainstream public through newspapers and magazines. Black people were outsiders to the academic side of the book publishing industry, essentially shut out. Black people created their own platforms, but those platforms haven't necessarily impacted mainstream America. Books published by Black presses weren't often found in many colleges and public schools.

Black Classic Books (1978), Dudley Randall's Broadside Press (1965), which later became Broadside Lotus Press in 2015, African World/Red Sea Press (1983), African American Images, Inc. (1980), and other small or single member presses have sprouted up over the years. Third World Press, founded in 1967 by Haki Madhubuti, Carolyn Rodgers and Johari Amini, grew—and at one time—was the largest Black-owned independent press in America. They published poetry, history books, and other topics across many genres, including African American Studies, education, women's studies, psychology and fiction. But Black publishers were not at the forefront when it came to textbook development and distribution. They were, and still today, significantly absent from many public schools and the STEM publishing arena (science, technology, engineering and math), where I spent some years as an editor.

White-owned STEM publishing houses published textbooks and serial works on many topics in academia, including general health, medical practice and nursing education. These publishers significantly impacted the strong moneymaking sectors of society by creating textbooks for STEM classes in colleges and trade schools. Sometimes that impact was negative. These medical textbooks, for example, included old myths and prejudiced information about Black culture and people. As a result, medical students were impacted, affecting how they treated Black patients. Many of these publishing institutions have existed since slavery, and those myths were foundational to the American education system. Publishers have not spent a great deal of time erasing structural racism from their creative process. When publishers don't include Black editors and authors in their publishing process, these myths and untruths remain unchecked. Often, the students who read these books believe and internalize what they were taught and carry that into their professions. This impacts how they teach, hire staff and practice medicine.

Black authors have written popular health-focused books in nutrition, skin care and general health, but white publishers manage the bulk of health education titles. Black publishing houses today lack the deep pockets larger white presses have and they have not enjoyed the centuries-old reputation white presses have maintained since the 1800s. Expanding further into STEM or other areas of academia where they can impact large student bodies may not be feasible. Publishers such as W.B. Saunders/Elsevier (1888), Lippincott Williams and Wilkins/Wolters Kluwer (1872), John Wiley and Sons (1807), Houghton Mifflin Harcourt (1832) and McGraw Hill (1836) were not going anywhere.

Universities and schools relied on books to teach and educate their student bodies, and university administrators have silently accepted the status quo. Meaning, committees at universities and school districts decided which books schools and colleges would adopt. Some of these relationships between publishers and schools were ironclad, making it possible for publishers to keep their books in schools and maintain consistent long-term annual sales. While major publishers were a part of this process, the smaller Black-owned presses were often neither part of the conversation nor producing the titles universities needed or wanted. What Black presses did have was strong support in their surrounding communities, but this support didn't often translate into national influence.

Philadelphia wasn't home to Black-owned presses like other cities—namely Baltimore, Detroit and Chicago. Philly nestled into a soulful Nouveau—strong and musical. We were an iconic city when it came to producing some of the most incredible musical artists and singers in America. My father's cousin, influenced by Harold Melvin and the Blue Notes, sang in a short-lived group, one of many Philly groups that either soared or remained unknown. We had hip-hop, visual arts, music and spoken word. My childhood experiences revolved around hip-hop, classical music, gospel songs and reading.

I loved books, music and art. They all represented multiple sides of the same coin and that coin always went with me, rustling in my pocket. Artistic mediums find a way to coexist. Reading and writing were the same way. Editing though required a certain rigidity. It demands but also finds its joy in developing and growing a text. It removes shade instead of basking in it. Editing for editing's sake is an art. There are many ways to define and interpret a word or a sentence. It's an art of rules usually bending to the will of one side. Editing can be fun and whimsical, even curating, but under the demands of corporate structure, it's something else.

## Yellow

Dandelions shoot up on lawns,
the sun shines down.
On my way to a yellow-bricked school,
while the wheels of the bus circle and turn.
Round and round, corner after corner,
Ink-circled dreams are etched in memory.
Planted seeds sprout underground,
as petals lay motionless 'til found.

## Chapter 1

# INK TO PAPER

## The Formative Years

The editing practice can be likened to attending an after-dark meeting. Editor and writer gather in a pitch-black alleyway where the writer feels comfortable and content wading in the innocence of blindness, imagining themselves gleaming and shining, creating carefree—writing to a captive, invisible audience. But that's how it is in the dark. It may feel eerie or smell odd, but nothing looks out of sorts in the dark because no one can see anything. But the "nothing" is what the editor is curious about. Editors shine in those spaces. We are the light. But there are three kinds of light: the kind that illuminates, the kind that feeds seeds and the kind that shines so bright it burns. Anyone can become an editor in some way, even if not a formally trained professional. Editors influence, set standards, lift up and champion, lead and direct. I realize today that I had met "editors" even before I was acquainted with the profession. I've felt their light. I've glistened under their shine. I've experienced growth and burned hands and times of no light at all.

One century before my birth, in 1871, freedom fighter Octavius Catto was murdered in Philadelphia. And one hundred years later, during a contentious point in Black woman's history—1977—the last year Elaine Brown served as chairwoman of the Black Panther Party and the year Assata Shakur was convicted—I was born. Childbirth and childhood are unpredictable. They are kaleidoscopes of changing colors and unpredictable patterns. You don't know when life will turn and plummet, rise and shift, rebound or break. Everything's unexpected when you're a child. Everything's new—no experience to draw from, no predictability. I was my parents' second and last child. My mom expected a rough birth, not a smooth one, a boy, and not a girl. I surprised my parents with both my gender and the ease with which I entered the world. I didn't cry; I looked around.

    I don't recall how old I was when I held my first book, but one of them reminded me of dingy blue jeans without

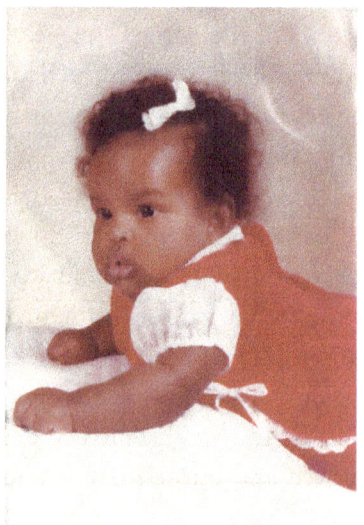

Three-month-old me.

Me, mom and my brother a few days after I was born.

stitched pockets, seams, zippers and hems. The frayed corners and inside pages felt tired like they had been on a long journey. My mom found the book at a local school book giveaway. When she handed it to me, I was sitting on a medium-planked oak wood floor in my bedroom. Illustrations of white children were inside along with the words *See Spot Run*.

Mom didn't concern herself with the age of the books and neither of my parents valued stuff over education. The more money was spent on high-priced items the less money they had for essentials like a savings account for college and paying the mortgage. They were staunch supporters of bargain hunting, sales, the dollar store and using what you had until it no longer worked. Bills were paid, we never went to bed hungry and clothes were purchased through layaway. I wore hand-me-downs until high school. We shopped cheap and stood in long welfare lines for cheese and no-frills food. My mom drove the same car until she couldn't drive it anymore.

My bother and I when I was an infant.

Pictured with my grandparents (mom's side); the only photo I have of them together.

After many years, her AMC Concord had no working back doors and the back windows didn't roll down. New furniture was rare. My parents only had two living room and dining room sets during their entire 50-plus years of marriage.

Reading before kindergarten was one of my mom's top goals and my dad read bedtime stories to me. Mom always had a vision for what her children's education would look like. She took advantage of every opportunity she had to give her children better. Her very name, Nadine, meant hope in French. Reading thrilled me. I would beg my parents for books anytime I saw them on PBS. Even though my parents weren't huge readers, they read newspapers. My parents were more into real-time information. They met through my mom's brother, my uncle Butch, who worked with my dad. Soon after, at age 21 and 23, the "Lion of Zion," Rev. Dr. Leon Sullivan, civil rights activist and founder of Sullivan Progress Plaza, the first shopping center in America owned and continually operated by African Americans, married my parents at Zion Baptist Church in 1970.

Both the *Philadelphia Inquirer* and the *Philadelphia Tribune* sat either on the sofa or the coffee table. Sunday mornings were for church services, and Sunday afternoons were for digesting information, eating to the sounds of TV chatter and coupon clipping. My dad, born and raised in North Philly, kept a bookcase in the hallway of our two-story row home in Mt. Airy, Philadelphia. Gracing its shelves were home repair books, *Roots* by Alex Haley, *Black Ice* by Eldridge Cleaver, Rita Dove's *Through the Ivory Gate*, *The Fisher King* by Paule Marshall, James Baldwin's *Another Country*, and old *Jet* magazines, among many other titles. The bookcase was also the shelf for any and everything else: pens, papers, bobby pins, a hairbrush or my dad's bowling and baseball trophies.

It was photo time, but clearly I was more interested in my book. LOL

Reading while mom styled my hair.

My mom, also from North Philly, wanted my brother and me to attend an elementary school that scored high in reading. She saw reading as foundational to getting a good education. It was such a sticking point that my mom followed school ratings published in the newspaper. The local paper listed the city's most achieving schools—the top elementary schools, middle schools, high schools, etc. One of the top elementary schools in the early '80s was in Northeast Philadelphia, a predominately white neighborhood. John Hancock Elementary Demonstration School scored high in reading and was one yellow school bus ride away. A Black woman principal led it for a while before she moved on to a different position within the School District of Philadelphia. Like other Black kids in Mt. Airy, I was bused to John Hancock, an elementary school planted in a different world, a world with more money.

The daily bus ride to the Northeast was rowdy. All the way to Hancock, kids were screaming and blasting their boom

Not sure if I was sleep or day dreaming.

boxes—singing "The Roof Is on Fire" and other hip-hop lyrics. I remember looking out the window and seeing how the neighborhood changed the farther away we ventured out of working-class Mt. Airy. The difference in housing stood out. The brick looked newer and street blocks were clean and tidy, like miniature model home neighborhoods. They were fresh like wet paint on a mural—shiny and dazzling. I sat struck with curiosity. Light reflected off houses and bounced around my head like future memories. I imagined myself living in one of those fancy row homes with their awnings, manicured lawns, cedar decks, and gorgeous pink flower trees the color of baby doll clothes. I was a fragile, six-year-old who didn't talk much. I was afraid to speak to people, tongue-tied even. My older brother had to step in sometimes. If I was in trouble, I went to him. One day a boy looked up my skirt, and I told my brother. He confronted the boy and that was that. It never happened again.

The schoolyard wasn't always safe for kids even when NTAs (nonteaching assistants) were present. I'd seen assaults and abuses that weren't reported or noticed. I was relieved I didn't have to fight. I had a big brother. In school I evaluated what was around me more than what I had to say about it. I thought more than I spoke. Looking out the window was easier than engaging with other kids. I didn't have many friends, so I appreciated the few I had and the pretty, shiny, new things I saw in this well-to-do neighborhood. I even tried to memorize the street names of where my favorite houses were so that I could remember them when I got older, but I soon realized—the people were not necessarily as lovely as the landscape.

John Hancock was modern and equipped with everything a child could want, from gymnastics equipment to musical instruments, to books. The library—where hardbacks and paperbacks seemed numerous and endless—held fantasies and secrets inside. Some days I'd wander into the school library, hunch down in the aisle and hide from the librarian. I didn't think the librarian liked me because she showed no interest in helping me. I felt uncomfortable, so I stayed hidden and explored on my own.

Books were stacked side by side and lined up on shelves that stretched across rooms and up walls. I entered a world of wonder. Libraries were a peaceful place, quiet, full of stories, and memories and the words of people alive in the present or alive in the great beyond. As a little girl, shy and awkward, I saw the library as a welcoming place of fun. I didn't have to socialize or talk to people or wait for other kids to figure out if I was cool. I could exist in a place of zero judgment. I could seek and find adventure. My elementary school library may have been small in size, but it was big to me in more ways than one. My place of refuge, my happy place. I usually gravitated toward poetry books. Mostly because they were short and I could read several poems in no time. This was a significant realization because I could only stay in the library for minutes, not hours.

On an ordinary day, I discovered Langston Hughes. There was nothing dramatic about this discovery. While alone, I pulled a random book off the shelf and began reading Langston Hughes's poetry. In no time I found myself going into the library looking for more of his poems. I didn't know he was Black, as I hadn't seen a picture of him, but maybe my soul knew. His words struck a chord and his thoughts seemed familiar. It was like he was talking to me, and I didn't need to say hello first. Reading didn't require bravery. I didn't need to be popular, pretty or "some type of way." All I had to do was open up a book. When I read the line "Life Ain't No Crystal Stair" from "Mother to Son," I thought, *yes, life ain't no crystal stair*. In six-year-old terms that meant happy times wouldn't always be happy. Fear made me less happy, but books made me subconsciously brave. I was brave in my head, in my imagination.

As a six-year-old, I had no knowledge of the Harlem Renaissance or the impact Langston Hughes had on the literary community or American life. I didn't learn much about his life or his complete body of work until I entered college. He was my first major introduction to the Black literary world. I started writing my own poetry and learned about different types of poems in school. My favorite classroom assignments were book reports and writing assignments. When I was 10, I learned diamanté—a seven-line, diamond-shaped poem. In one of my writing assignments, I wrote about growth and transformation—life coming out of the ground. A seed. In hindsight, I may have written about a seed because I dreamed of growing up. I didn't particularly like being a child, not because I was abused, because I wasn't, but because I was a child paralyzed by fear. I didn't like being afraid all the time. I wanted to be a grownup because I thought grownups weren't afraid. My diamanté poem from the fifth grade:

Seed<br>
Small, smooth,<br>
Digging, planting, waiting,<br>
Water, sun, growth, development,<br>
Expanding, changing, picking,<br>
Soft, silky,<br>
Flower

Reading this poem as an adult, I think about how remarkable nature is. Seeds always become something else when they are planted. They don't fear or experience the emotional baggage of humanity. They just grow. The seed waits to be planted, to be loved by the sun, and touched by the rain. Then, the seed is forgotten and the flower is all that remains. When it withers, more seeds are planted. As a child, I loved flowers and anything pretty and soft. The transformation of a seed from small, firm and unnoticed to a long slender burst of color was fascinating. The flower blooms toward the end of its journey. I pretended the seed was me. Every time I read this poem, I am reminded that the end of a journey is meant to be beautiful, and like any child, I wanted to be beautiful.

This poem won a school-wide poetry contest—go figure. As the winner for my grade level, I remember being ecstatic, but I was even more thrilled that I didn't have to read it in front of an auditorium full of people. Throughout elementary school I continued to read poetry but didn't write poems outside of school back then. My environment was full of other artsy activities like art camp and museum visits. I would see childhood friends reading Judy Blume on occasion, but we never got together to form a kid's book club or anything like that. It didn't cross my mind or anyone else's. Reading and writing were always solitary. As a child, music was the easiest way for me to fit in—choir was community. Since Philly was a musical city, many of my friends could sing. We would sing in stairwells, hallways, buses or anywhere. Philadelphia public schools offered opportunities to perform inside and outside of school. When I wasn't alone, I was usually with my singing friends.

The playground was home to hopscotch, stepping, kids racing other kids, Numbers, suicide (handball), Ms. Mary Mack and other games. Among friends, I was reliable and quiet. Even though I didn't get into stepping, I was a pro at turning double Dutch. They counted on me for that. The rope was never "flickted" in my hands. We chanted,

"Challenge, Challenge 1, 2, 3, 4…" as we jumped rope. Outside of school I sang in the children's choir at church. I loved to sing even though I didn't enjoy being in front of people. Being with others made singing in front of people easier. Even when introduced to the viola, I had other violinists and viola players surrounding me. The music community was my community. Books, music and art camp filled my childhood. Music was a strong influence.

My introduction to the viola occurred in the first grade. At the time I was interested in the violin and had never heard of the viola—an instrument that looked similar to the violin, but sang a deeper song, a full bodied and unassuming sound. The only violin in the entire school was so little it was given to the smallest girl in the class. The rest of us were given violas. We first learned to play "Old MacDonald Had a Farm." Our teacher asked me to play it in front of our small strings class. I was terrified to play out of unison, as an individual. It didn't matter how lovely someone thought I sounded. After he taught us "Twinkle, Twinkle Little Star," he left the school, and I thought my viola/violin journey ended there. When the next strings teacher finally came, I went to see if I could return to learning the violin. The new violin teacher held an impromptu audition the same day I asked her and I failed. After that, I remember her happy voice telling me she wouldn't teach me. She seemed relieved. The experience shattered my confidence and encouraged me to stay in the background instead of going after what I wanted.

Church, on the other hand, provided comfort and reprieve. As a little girl, it's where I would come to develop the little courage I had. My Sunday school teachers, Mrs. Matthews and Mrs. Ferne Hart, were encouraging and gentle. Class took place on the second floor of an old beige stucco-styled building. The stairwell led the way through darkness, and the sound of my black patent leather shoes hitting the concrete steps echoed. The blunt sound was louder than I wanted. As my church shoes clanked on the concrete, it felt like I was marching to *The Twilight Zone* theme song. At the top of the stairs, the heat kicked in, and behind the push-open doors were the smiles of my Brown-Black and Light-Black Sunday school teachers. I grew attached to them. After kindergarten, I tried to sneak back into Mrs. Matthews' class. Mrs. Ferne noticed me right away. I didn't think she would notice because I was so timid and often went unnoticed at elementary school. Her sweet voice said, "Shana, you're not in this class anymore." My little heart deflated into a collapsed ball of jumping confetti. I didn't want to move on. I liked the comfort of staying put—the familiar.

I didn't realize that staying put didn't mean change wouldn't happen. I didn't grasp the inevitability of change occurring even if you don't move. Perpetual comfort was an illusion. My Sunday school teacher was a living, breathing being, not a fixture, not static. People move and grow. Everything moves and grows and changes, even tragically. I was seven when I heard about her death. She and her husband were murdered in their home over a business dispute between the killers and her husband. The killers were convicted and sent to death row. I don't remember the church ever speaking of her after that. There was no grieving process that I can recall. It was a silence I didn't understand as a little person.

One year later I watched the 1985 MOVE bombing on our small turn-dial TV in the dining room. In West Philly, a stand off between MOVE members (a communal activist group) and the police took place at 6221 Osage Avenue. Five children died. I remember the sirens and the flames on rooftops. A Philly kid sees a lot in childhood, and you never know if you'll end up a witness or a victim. Children throw themselves into whatever they're surrounded by to deal with what they've seen, experienced or survived—art, fights, isolation, drugs, overachievement, church, sports, etc. Book reports and choir rehearsals were my thing. Elementary school grew my relationship with words. I didn't realize loving books or writing could lead to something greater—like an actual career path.

Middle school introduced me to more options. In the heart of North Philly at Thirteenth and Susquehanna—in the middle of the hood, where academics and muggers lived side by side—stood AMY 2 (Alternative to the Middle Years) middle school. In contrast to my elementary school, it sat in a neighborhood of less money and less fancy. Big in talent, intelligence and determination, it was only a few steps away from Temple University. Located inside an older run-down building, AMY's schoolyard was open and welcoming to both petty thieves and passersby. We were unfazed by the thieves who would come through and rob us of our earrings and anything easily accessible. That was everyday school life. Uncommon to other schools, class choice or being able to pick your classes, was normal. I took classes in Spanish, foreign language and architecture. Middle school was full of self-discovery. Every class seemed to ask, "What do you want out of life?" "Who do you want to be?"

I felt so motivated I decided to go back to studying the violin. I asked my middle school strings teacher if she would teach me, and she said yes without an audition. After a few months of private lessons, I played violin in the citywide middle school orchestra. I also sang in the school choir, marched in the Thanksgiving Day parade and wrote fiction. Students were able to shadow college students and learn more about the college experience. I shadowed an architecture student at Temple University. Our principal, Dr. Eugene Richardson, was an original Tuskegee Airman and he arranged many partnerships for the school, which made it possible to learn about various fields of study. Middle school took me on a journey and I dreamed until high school.

I didn't receive this same level of career exploration in grades nine to twelve. High school was completely different. It was stricter, and my now 14-year-old self was introduced to a world of achieving generalized academic excellence. No more wondering, or dreaming, or becoming, or exploring one's passion. It was time to work. When I got to high school, the educational landscape was more regimented. I attended an all-girls college-prep high school—The Philadelphia High School for Girls founded in 1848. It was the first public high school for young women in Pennsylvania. It was, THE Girls' High, a school, which had a reputation for graduating powerful women leaders, such as C. Delores Tucker, Elaine Brown and Constance Clayton. Entrance was heavily based on test scores. Even though my grades were high, I had to submit several letters of recommendation to get into Girls' High. Academic performance, student work, extracurricular activities or interviews wasn't enough to be accepted in 1991.

Test scores were key to receiving opportunities. If a student didn't have high test scores, it was an uphill battle to prove that the student was worthy of the opportunity, or in this case, worthy of entering a highly ranked college-prep high school. Getting into any of Philadelphia's premiere public college-prep high schools—Girls' High, Central, Julia Masterman, etc.—was like a badge of honor. Once I got in, there was a strong focus on college acceptance. Although I benefited greatly from their focus on leadership and academic excellence, the classes were standard and focused entirely on preparing students for higher education. Instead of more classes in language or architecture or engineering, only standard courses in world history, American history, Spanish, English, art, social studies and math (algebra, trig and elementary functions) were available.

The only unique classes I recall were Black history and Chinese. Outside of those, the classes were a part of the traditional curriculum all public high school students received. It was quite the adjustment transitioning from middle school to high school. In high school student work was mostly based on college prep, and college education was tied to leadership. We valued sisterhood and we were being groomed for civic, societal and even cultural leadership as women. The model, as I saw it, was foundational and not career specific. I didn't pick up where I left off. I went from being fairly engaged in middle school to barely getting by in high school, and my low-grade testing abilities were a dark cloud looming over me.

Girls' High—known for sending over 90 percent of students to college. It was a given that a "Girls' High girl" would further her education. There was no escaping that and other alternatives didn't even enter my head. My parents were emphatic about the college path. College was the golden ticket to success (that and good credit). The curriculum was rigorous, and when I started my four-year journey, I was in complete denial about how much work I had to put in. When I came home from school, all I wanted to do was draw, write, read, play the piano, practice for my violin recital or go to choir rehearsal—anything but schoolwork.

I was deeper into music then, and my violin teacher was a string specialist who had played with the Philadelphia Orchestra, a "Big Five" orchestra. She had a will of steel.

"I'm full-blooded Italian," she said to us one day. "These women today cry over any and everything. My sisters and I went to my aunt's funeral last week and not one of us cried. Not one. "

*Was that comment supposed to be a pep talk or make the three of us in her class more determined or disciplined?* Brilliant and stern she showed more strength than acquiescence. She wanted us to succeed whether we liked her or not. During every class, our teacher would bang on the keys of her piano as she played along with us. She played piano, violin and viola and would yell at us every time we played a too flat or too sharp note. When we did, she told us to start from the beginning. For one of her recitals, we practiced her arrangement of Nat King Cole's *Unforgettable*. A difficult arrangement, our practice brought out the grit in us. It was 100% will—not creative or divine. Playing music or singing can be such a spiritual thing, like channeling the essence of God. You let go. When we mastered her arrangement, we weren't angelic, just relieved. It was like we were training to be tough.

She imbued force. Her blond hair grazed her shoulders and laid neat. Straw like, it looked like layers of corn silk ripped from the stalk and fried on the edges. Her roots were dark like her penciled in eyebrows and she dressed like a retired bargain hunter only concerned with the perfect performance of her students. One day she talked about feeling what you play and she let go and moved from side to side, not looking at her fingers or anyone else. She closed her eyes and played. In that moment I was reminded of the first time I saw a violinist rock my senses and elevate every cell in my body. She was a gospel violinist that went to my church—Katherine Burton. She ministered all over the city and the precision and soul with which she played stamped "blessed" imprints on every heart that heard her. Not only did she move her body, she would dip down into a seated position while playing. Her signature style attracted large crowds to every concert.

Although Mrs. Kathy's performance was its own fete, my teacher's musical rendition reminded me of my love for the violin and how I wanted to develop my own style. Under our teacher's methods, I caught a glimpse of glory, but couldn't rest in the everlasting like her and Katherine Burton and just play. Let go and play. Instead my class was more caught up in the time and patience needed to practice. Music can take up your entire life. My Achilles heel was sight-reading and I struggled with vibrato. She told us, "make sure the joints of your fingers are relaxed and that you're holding your instrument firmly." *How do I relax with her?* Instead I was determined to place my finger in the exact spot needed to avoid out-of-tune notes. Her methods albeit strict gave us glowing reviews from Joseph Simon, the supervisor at Philly's division of music education. In a 1992 memorandum from the School District of Philadelphia he remarked, "the young musicians played consistently well in tune."

Learning how to read music and play different arrangements helped me read books faster, helped me think. The techniques and playing positions from saddle to forth were invaluable lessons, but playing the violin soon became a job—*perform well and get selected to play in the recital*. Being chosen didn't feel as good as it should have. The violin became more about mastery and less about the soul and feel of music. Exhaustion set in. I wasn't feeling or enjoying the music. I was executing. I couldn't let go and play. It felt like passing a performance test. And standardized testing brought me even lower.

Standardized testing was a significant low point in the evolution of the American education system and in the evolution of myself. It didn't determine how successful or smart of a student I was. Although my low and mediocre test scores didn't hold me back entirely, they limited opportunities to some extent. Schools are conditioned to believe that if you don't test well, you are academically incompetent. Testing is supposed to test competence, but I think it's just another oppressive tool designed to create barriers. My mom noticed my falling test scores back in elementary school and took me to a nationally known tutoring center. It wasn't cheap, and I now recognize just how much of a sacrifice that was because we were working-class poor and the tutors weren't even skilled enough to help me.

My parents invested heavily in their children. Despite this, there was virtually no change in my standardized testing scores. The tutors were nice, but their methods didn't work. In a testing environment, I interpreted questions and answers differently. Plus, I lacked concentration, and it didn't help that I didn't think like the test. Expert test-taking was a learned behavior. The only way to learn that is to spend a good amount of time taking tests and learning the rationales behind the correct answers. Advanced test-taking skills are usually taught at the collegiate and graduate level. I don't recall getting much of that in elementary, middle or high school. Teachers taught content, not test-taking skills.

I struggled to stay engaged and the standardized testing curse didn't go away. I attended PSAT classes in high school and at Temple University and still scored low on the SAT. I didn't know how to solve this issue and would ease my frustration by reading. Reading and writing were my great escapes. Sometimes I would skip lunch and go to the library and wander. I'd sit down and read W.E.B. Du Bois, or other historical or African American Studies books, such as *Black Women in White America: A Documentary History* by Gerda Lerner. At that time I wanted to know more about Black women, Black composers and other topics not covered in class.

Meanwhile, I sang with my choir all over Philadelphia. As a soprano with Joy Unlimited Youth Mass Choir, we sang at churches with other groups, community events and gospel choir competitions. We sang at least every other weekend. My attention settled more on outside activities. As a result, I was failing in some classes and many of my teachers were just as disengaged as I was. My lack of focus didn't help the situation, but in the end, I still graduated. Fortunately, my performing arts classes in school choir and orchestra saved my GPA from catastrophe. My creative activities paved the way to college. Thank God for the arts.

Despite the ups and downs, Girls' High left behind a piece of itself. There was an ever-present energy that said women were to be heard and meant to lead in any or all places. It was a push forward. Girls' High girls were meant to influence. As a Girls' High student, there weren't any classes such as home economics, wood shop or typing. There was an atmosphere of "more." Being a good cook wasn't enough, and building with one's hands wasn't as impactful as conquering systems. And as for typing, it re-enforced the narrative that women were supporters, not leaders. Women were more than what we were pidgin-holed into. Black women throughout history taught every Black girl through self-publishing, speeches, writing, activism, and building schools and institutions that women can soar beyond predetermined roles. We were the ones that could go beyond. Even though I didn't have the best grades, I knew I could go beyond. I wouldn't be someone to push aside, but someone to be lifted up. In the 1994 edition of Girls' High's *Calliope,* a poem from one of my classmates Robynn Pitts captures it well, "I am me. I am an individual, like no other. I am not obligated to conform to the standards of another. I am free." After graduation, I enrolled as an undeclared undergraduate at Penn State University.

### College and Collages

Colors press against soles, and gold leaves glint orange.
Dry grass and the fresh fallen, hide paths and cover feet.
But as the wind lifts them high, higher than waving tassels,
they disintegrate into brilliant, bold flecks of hope and light.
As time layers upon itself, possibilities land soft,
and the ground is seen, again and again and again.

## Chapter 2

# NITTANY LIONS AND LITERARY GIANTS

## A Brave New Collegiate World

In the fall, central Pennsylvania turns into an amazing color-steeped wonderland. A cross-country drive from Philly to State College was mythic-magical. The vivid yellows, oranges and reds transformed a bland, green forest into a vibrant landscape. It turned any long drive into a spectacular horticultural tour, an advanced course in natural wonder. In late August I arrived at Penn State. The leaves and trees were still ordinary then, but I would witness this lit escapade every fall during Greyhound bus rides back to Philly. I was happy to attend college. I made it. My hard work paid off. I was relieved that I didn't need to develop a plan B for my life. My continued happiness though was a little uncertain. College was like receiving a surprise birthday cake. You look forward to the celebration but are unsure about the event itself. Is this a sweet cake or a dry, stale surprise?

My early years at Penn State were filled with the usual classes I had in high school—physics, English, some form of math, etc. By the time I graduated from high school, I was convinced becoming an engineer or architect was what I wanted, mostly because I was exposed to the idea in middle school. The idea of building and designing was always appealing to me. Even though Girls' High had some extracurricular publishing activities students could engage in (the *Iris Newspaper* and *Calliope*), I didn't learn about book publishing and editing until I got to Penn State.

Once I started taking serious writing courses, I became more interested in the English degree program, which eventually led me to book editing. After I declared my major, I completed three concentrations—African American literature, creative writing and publishing. Editing was a checkpoint for writers as they brought their written works to a press for public consumption. Writers take their ideas or concepts and express them using words, which become sentences, then paragraphs, which make up chapters that form manuscripts, and at the end of it all, a printer merges pages with a spine and cover, creating a bound book.

It is, in fact, like building, fashioning and pottery making. Once light shines on a manuscript, shaping begins, just as a sculptor takes clay and shapes it into something, anything. The clay could be one formless blob (a piece of disorganized prose) or a figure with no definition or identity (well-written content that lacks focus), or a clear shape that lacks polish (good content littered with spelling and grammatical errors). Editing transforms or improves, and every work needs some form of shaping or styling.

Sometimes when I read smooth, impeccable writing, I wonder how much of that is excellent untouched writing and how much of that is exceptional editing. My favorite African American writers were smooth and lyrical, and in the era of slavery and reconstruction, there were no prominent book editors I could name, just Black authors and printers.

However all that writing came into existence, I appreciated the soulfulness and rhythm of Black writing of all ages. The poetry, the essays, the novels and the way words danced on pages—the syncopation, the crescendo, the decrescendo and keeping time with words mixed with punctuation.

Growing up in a musical city, I heard beats and rhythm in everything, everywhere—while walking, while listening to the radio, when standing in line waiting for food. If you listen, you can even hear rhythm in Black speeches, in theatrical monologues, and in everyday discussions. I heard Maya Angelou once call it Sweet Language, La Lang Douce—the inflection and the drawing out of words. "Hey, how are you doing," becomes "Heeey, how are you doooing?" You can put Black language on sheet music. When I began my English degree program at Penn State, I didn't know that Penn State was one of the few universities that offered an African American literature emphasis. Grateful for this, I dove right in but quickly realized that the rules and standards were tug and pull—my feel for language, the rhythm I'd hear didn't want to adapt to the rules of standardized English.

But adaptation was a huge part of the college experience. I tucked away the tug and pull as I explored the deep intricacies of language itself. Learning to write and edit, I wore both the beanie of a writer and the top hat of an editor. It was beneficial to have this balance because it was key to understanding how a writer feels about someone reviewing, critiquing and handling their work. I couldn't be a writer without studying the craft and learning to use various literary forms such as metaphor and alliteration, poetry and varied points-of-view, etc. A good writer doesn't just automatically become a great editor. It required compartmentalizing and detaching myself from the text or objectively handling the author's words without inserting myself, without taking ownership. But many amazing editors never write books, and many writers never learn how to edit.

Penn State University, a predominately white college nestled in central Pennsylvania, was not known for racial acceptance and diversity. A few high school classmates remarked on the disgraceful treatment of Black students when Penn State first integrated. I felt uneasy, but I couldn't ignore how the recruiters pursued me despite my roller-coaster academic record. I couldn't turn down a state grant and in-state tuition. Penn State was a bargain. Although I visited several HBCUs, they were expensive, and I was not a candidate for a scholarship due to my mediocre test scores. Scholarship money mostly went to Black students who performed well on their SATs. Plus, when researching schools, I only checked out engineering programs.

All the HBCUs with engineering programs were too far south and I wanted to stay in Pennsylvania. Lincoln and Cheney were not on my radar because I was unfamiliar with their engineering programs. If I knew I'd become an English major, an HBCU would've made better sense—more Black professors, more Afrocentric teaching, more mentorship opportunities and better academic advising. Thankfully, my Black professors at Penn State left an impression. As a result, I wasn't groomed or expected to assimilate or embrace white interpretations of what good writing should be without critique. My most significant influence was Dr. Bernard W. Bell, a Black English professor from South Bronx, New York and a Marine. He was the head of the African American Literature program and the late Sterling Brown, a poet, mentored him. The author of *The Afro-American Novel and Its Tradition*, Dr. Bell's classes laid the foundation for how I interpreted and understood Black literature, Black life. It helped shape my approach and initiated my evolution as a Black woman editor.

At Penn State, I was immersed in African American, British and American literature. As an English major, I was required to take British literature (up to 1798), along with Jane Austen, T.S. Eliot, Chaucer, Laurence Sterne, Jane Austen, Gertrude Stein, Frances Burney, Seamus Heaney, and others. In the African American literature emphasis, there was Slavery and the Literary Imagination and African American Folk Tradition. Liberation (also known as slave) narratives were foundational to understanding Afro-American literature and interpreting the recurring themes and elements present in African American stories—the five residual oral forms present in Black literature (oratory, song, myth, legend and tale) noted by Dr. Bell; signifying as described in Dr. Henry Louis Gates' *The Signifying Monkey* and the blues expressed through Dr. Houston A. Baker, Jr.'s work *Blues, Ideology, and Afro-American Literature: A Vernacular Theory*.

For Dr. Bell to be in a tenured position at Penn State, speaking openly to predominately white classes about the horrors of both slavery and oppression, was quite the lesson in unwavering confidence. Daily, he chipped away at the ignorance white students naturally lived in—an unaware and unchallenged consciousness. This kind of teaching needed to be there. If you placed him in an HBCU, he would have empowered Black students while preaching to the choir. At Penn State, he was a beacon of information and a champion of freedom and agency. He always stood, as a force, a literary giant who walked back straight, marching across campus in a crisp hat and a sweeping taupe trench coat. I didn't possess that bravery back then. I could tell that many of the white students were uncomfortable hearing and reading about slavery, especially in our Slavery and Literary Imagination class.

Although Black students were more connected to these stories and had a general understanding, most white students were shielded and didn't hear much about slavery. Both groups of students though (white and Black) sat in class wanting to disconnect from slavery. No one wanted to wade into it as deep as we would.

Uncomfortable for everyone, classes tackled the meaning of institutionalized slavery, what it meant to be enslaved and the character of the slaveholder. This teaching was foundational in revealing the power of Black stories written under the boot of enslavement and pseudo-freedom or freedom with restrictions and sanctions. We were free to entertain and serve and not free to gain political and economic power. In liberation narratives, African Americans used paper and pen in their fight for liberty, showcasing their humanity, their love, their genius and their oratorical ability to persuade. Slaveholders were adamant about stopping Africans from learning how to read. For example, the state legislature passed a law in Alabama demanding that enslaved Africans receive one hundred lashes if they were taught to read and write. This fear-based idea fed into the narrative that Black people would rise and position themselves as equal to whites, eventually overpowering them. The enslaved threatened the oppressor's quest for perpetual domination. So when enslaved Africans learned to read, write and publish, they accessed avenues that would pave the way to elusive freedom.

Slavery was, essentially, meant to be a way of life. Not an event in history, but a model—now and in the future. White slaveholders and the supporting community needed to keep Black people below them as a permanent underclass to sustain an economy built on slave labor, producing soft and sweet—cotton and sugar. Cotton, which would be used to make paper and sugar, would drive the confectionery industry. Slave labor was essentially connected to everything. For African Americans—a class of people pushed to serve, and not to think for themselves, live for themselves or serve their own interests. Freedom was a dangerous concept for the white slaveholder, so restrictions, such as making it illegal to teach an enslaved person to read, were essential. African American writing promoted agency and control over one's sense of reason.

While Africans were blocked from owning land, they were unchaining their minds. Works such as *Incidents in the Life of A Slave Girl* by Harriet Jacobs, *The Narrative of Frederick Douglass*, *Black Poets* edited by Dudley Randall, *Our Nig* by Harriet E. Wilson, *The Autobiography of An Ex-Colored Man* by James Weldon Johnson, *The Conjure Woman* by Charles Chestnutt, *Invisible Man* by Ralph Ellison, *Train Whistle Guitar* by Albert Murray, *The Chaneysville Incident* by David Bradley, *Their Eyes Were Watching God* by Zora Neale Hurston were some of the titles on the list of books we read and analyzed.

*Invisible Man* was the greatest work of American literature—as was told to me by every English professor I ever had, white and Black. My first thought when I first began reading it was my connection to the idea of being *invisible*—not being seen or noticed. It reminded me of how I felt as a Black child, but in my own experiences—going to a white school in the Northeast and my various interactions with racism. I had a few white teachers who didn't seem to like Black children, treating them like they didn't matter, like they were *invisible*. I'm not sure those teachers appreciated the influx of Black children coming from all sides of Philly. The Northeast was not diverse or particularly welcoming in the '80s. But I also had white teachers who embraced teaching Black children. It was a mixed bag. You never knew who was going to like you.

There was also this sense of concealment beyond the throes of invisibility. I felt hidden like a seed covered by soil and darkness. Being concealed in daily life is often about blocked views due to neighboring circumstances or distractions. Just as my invisibility was interpreted as this feeling of non-existence, being unseen was about being under shadows or behind other kids, events and noise. I felt present but not always noticed. But I didn't necessarily want to be seen all the time. That could be a good thing and a bad thing. People recognize the good in you or "see you" so much that you end up in the middle of their drama. For the most part, people would see me and call me "quiet." But I was only the "quiet" one because everyone else was loud.

Reading books like *Invisible Man*, *Beloved* and *The Chaneysville Incident* was particularly difficult. In high school, slavery was a mere blip in the coverage of American history, so I was unprepared. The anger bubbled up from the pit of my stomach like rotten cotton candy laced with spoiled eggs. Reading the torture, pain and horrifying daily struggles of Black men, women and children was a harrowing experience. I didn't know much about my family's slavery experience in South Carolina and Virginia. If I closed my eyes and imagined South Carolina, I pictured a state overflowing with bleeding cotton, soaking red balls of it covering the streets, tucked under railroads and stretched out under graves. There was nothing clean, white or soft about my vision.

I wasn't aware of many details. There was no family griot around to relay the full story. But I knew my paternal great-grandfather Abraham Murph and my great-grandmother Rubel (nickname Ruby) and her brothers and sisters left South Carolina for Philly. Per the census, Rubel left behind four deceased siblings: Eugene, Squire, Grady and Samuel. My mother's side was no less complicated. My maternal great-grandmother, Mattie, worked as a maid for a Jewish family in Philadelphia and gave birth to two children—one daughter, my grandmother, and one son—whereabouts unknown. My great-grandmother had no birth certificate and asking my family questions left me with more questions. How many siblings did Grandpop Abraham have? How did Grandmom Mattie get to Philly from Virginia? Information was scant and scattered, obituaries were incomplete and the census was only slightly helpful. Tracing genealogy requires a certain amount of relentlessness.

The closest thing my family had to a griot was my dad tracking our family's timeline through events captured on camera, stills and video—family gatherings, parties, births, vacations, visits, trips to the zoo, holidays, birthdays with my cousins and even my laughter as a toddler. That was the record. Several boxes of home videos and photos were stored in closets. My father was the oldest of nine children and his mother Ruth, was born in Philadelphia to parents who migrated from Calhoun County, South Carolina. She grew up under her mother's entrepreneurial spirit. Grandma Ruby owned a store in North Philly. Because Ruth died of bone cancer when I was ten, I was too young to know her well. I just remember her as a force to be reckoned with and a fierce card player who one day gave me a small green patent leather change purse with a five-dollar bill inside. When she was lying in a hospital bed at Jefferson Hospital, I recall being bothered that I didn't really know her, and that the doctors didn't seem to do much or care for her.

My mom's mom, Isabell, on the other hand, was with me for my entire childhood. She was the daughter of parents from West Virginia and Virginia who never married. Raised by her stepmother and Holiness preacher father, she didn't have a happy childhood. She often told me how cruel

Standing with my Great Grandmom Ruby and her friends at Raymond Rosen Projects in North Philly. I was three-years-old.

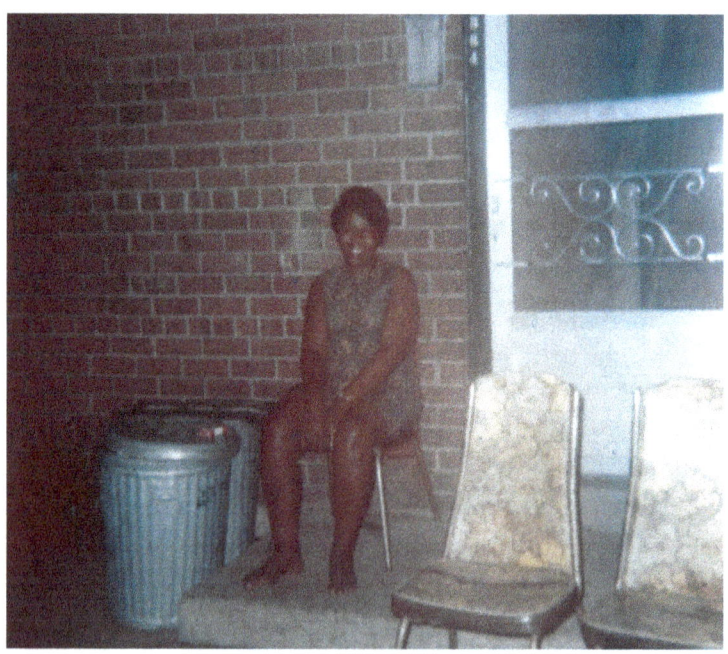

Grandmom Ruth Murph Salley (dad's side).

her stepmother was. How she would beat her just because. Forced to drop out of William Penn High School (an all-girls school at the time), she had to work at the dry cleaner her father owned until one day she caught the eye of my biological grandfather, George. After one look, he wanted to marry her. I only met him once, at his brother's church in West Philly (where my uncle was the founding pastor). An alcoholic and an abuser, my grandmother divorced him when my mom was little. Afterward, Isabell married my grandfather Clyde. They remained married until my grandfather died of cancer when I was 13.

Although I don't remember meeting my grandmother's mother Mattie, my bother remembers us visiting her when she was sick and bedridden. We walked up the stairs of my grandparents house in Willingboro, NJ and peaked into the back room to say hi. I've always been curious about her life. I have one of her only possessions, a small one-cabinet end table I keep in my bedroom. She was a tall, stocky, light-skinned Black woman raised by her father after her mother died. Her family was scattered. I was told that her mother was Native American, but her clan affiliation was unknown. Only traces of Native heredity remain in my genetics (1% per my Ancestry DNA test). Finding a record of her brief marriage and other records regarding her siblings and parents was an undertaking. School or work heavily occupied my time, so connecting the dots that stitched my genes together would have to wait.

Even though, as an undergraduate, I dove into the lives of others, each retelling was palpable and timeless and not a "back then" experience. I felt the despair. Every scream from enslaved ancestors is in the DNA of every living descendent—much of that trauma is still clearly visible in the coping mechanisms Black families used to move forward beyond the various forms of slavery and systems of oppression still thriving today. Black authors like Frederick Douglass were coming out of slavery and telling their stories so they could tear down this institutional antebellum system of unimaginable cruelty. This made literacy dangerous for the slaveholder. Literacy and reading were catalysts for change—a change in circumstances, an opportunity. As a result, the public torture of children, women and men was implemented to steer Black people away from rebellion and revolt—and yet we revolted with a nonstop relentless fight.

To read was to think; white supporters and pleased beneficiaries of slavery wanted Black people to do neither. Many whites needed Black people to fully internalize what various white groups wanted them to believe—they were incapable of learning; they were subhuman, immoral, insensitive to pain, and imbeciles. If slaveholders started allowing Black people to read, they'd risk losing the upper hand. What if Black people thought they were as good as white people? Once educated, the enslaved will seek what white people have—freedom, land, wealth and control. When any group attempts to build a permanent underclass, they have to control every aspect of the oppressed person's life. What they eat or taste, and how they think, feel, hear, smell and see. They must seek to control the brain, the body, and all five senses. With slavery, slaveholders were essentially creating a road map to a society where the advantage always leaned toward the dominant group, which grew stronger and stronger over time.

To ensure that white people stayed wealthy, privileged and powerful in government and business, there must first be complete control over the Black body and Black ambitions. This control must be so extensive that there's allegiance to the established system, even if it's subconscious. The only path toward true freedom is to control how he or she interprets what's seen, heard, smelled, touched, and tasted. If not, enslavement doesn't end with the death of the enslaved person; it creates a legacy of mental enslavement. Black people had to pivot and fight to keep moving forward. When the enslaved saw torture, shackles, the bound feet of children, the amputations of the defiant, the consequences of freedom-seeking and the inevitability of mental breakdown, the response was to fight for bravery and still strive for freedom. When the enslaved heard the crack of the whip, the sounds of wailing, the humming of hope's song and not the realization of victory's chorus, the response was the singing of a procession leading the walk to freedom.

When the enslaved smelled sweat and soil and burning flesh from branded skin and the dried blood of healing wounds, the response was to grab the flowers all around and smell beauty and notice the color purple. When the enslaved tasted the sour bitterness of starvation—dry and tart like rotting leather or food left over from the slaveholder's table, the response was soul food—a style of cooking that made anything taste good. When what the enslaved touched belonged to someone else—the face (every expression), arms (holding babies ripped away in an instant), legs (between and beneath), hair (bound in plaits and covered), torso (not allowed to protect or shelter), and back (the whipping post), the response was to touch the slim body of a pen and write. Writing is a form of control. Taking what has been seen, smelled, heard, felt and tasted to build molds and shapes out of pain, laying it down brick by brick to form a road to walk on, where the end of the walk is better and more beautiful. When people do not reinterpret what they see, smell, feel, touch and taste, they are impacted by whoever is in control.

Reading and writing—two practices holding hands like soldiers pursuing freedom. African Americans asserted their humanity, used their ability to reason, expressed desires and showed off their intellect. The literature of Frederick Douglass, David Ruggles, Sojourner Truth and others supported and propelled the fight for freedom and humanity forward. The anguish on these pages led the way to the Thirteenth Amendment. All this writing and reading gave me so much insight. I was introduced to not only the pain of my existence, but the hope of it, and seeing beyond what was in front of me. Black writers had vision. Surviving slavery and the aftermath of reconstruction and Jim Crow was about hope. As I was being set free from ignorance, I eyeballed the world with a squint as my soul opened up. I was now aware of how much the world could hate me and how much I could overcome it.

## Tight Shoes

Rushing to step out
The closet bears no opinion
Grab a shirt and pull-up jeans
Slip-on bangles and press-in shoes
Notice the reflection opposite the mirror
Cramped feet under straps of leather
Second thoughts, third thoughts, shoes flung high
I walked out barefoot and left without a sigh

## Chapter 3

# CONFORMING TO STYLE

### Learning How to Edit

The world of artists beams with gifted talent. But I never saw a financial benefit to being an artist full time. I enjoyed writing, but scribbling on paper—whether to create pictures or paragraphs—was art, and artists may or may not make much money. Even if they do, beginnings could be humble. Without dressy heals or stacks of bills, I could be left with only change in my pocket and that giddy feeling of a smile gone wild in my spirit. Art gave life but did art support life? I'd always been encouraged by my parents to go the way of financial security. Engineering careers paved a path to home ownership. *What do writing salaries yield?*

As I finished my concentrations in writing and African American Literature, I saw myself as an essayist, a poet and a short story writer. Short writing was easier to manage. I could complete a short work in a limited period of time without feeling stressed out or overwhelmed. My pen felt light and airy when I wrote a short piece. It felt like a petal skipping along short, smooth branches, falling and rising with the wind unconscious of limitations. Short stories were fun and completed in 20 pages or less. Long-form or book writing was more involved, whether fiction or nonfiction. But I decided to pivot away from writing temporarily. I wanted to challenge myself and learn everything there was to know about book publishing.

Although I briefly held an interest in journalism, it became apparent that the journalism majors graduating from Penn State had trouble finding work. There were more journalists than there were open positions in newspapers and magazines. Blogs were not a thing then, and the Internet was still new. There were Black editors in mass communication, but I didn't gravitate toward it. I marveled at a journalist's passion and quest for the full story. Being in journalism meant I would have access to Black reporters and Black magazine editors, which would've been a huge plus.

The world of newspapers and magazines had diversity. African Americans maintained a significant presence in journalism for centuries. But my perception of communication positions in corporate America was fast-paced chaos and long hours, completing hours of investigative reporting, researching and extensive interviewing. Although I didn't completely dislike getting assigned a story, I was in love with the craft of writing itself and writing what I wanted to write about. I embraced research, but more so as a part of the book-writing process. The important reporting work was best left for news-driven writers who enjoyed the "big story" chasing environment and real-time investigation. As a moderately introverted person, the thought of working in a news setting seemed too chaotic. I pictured myself running frantic, with bags under my eyes and coffee stains on my wash-and-wear, poly-blend sweater.

Unlike journalism majors, English majors were being hired everywhere. It was a degree that was attractive in many different sectors. English majors worked as teachers, went on to become lawyers, worked as literary agents, became technical writers, or served as book editors, project managers, etc. It's a degree that transfers easily into many fields. Employers often saw English degrees as a solid base-level skillset. As an English major, I was being taught to write, analyze, solve problems and think critically. English degrees had broad appeal. I confirmed my decision when I decided to write for a small campus newspaper as a sophomore. I later served as a design assistant for *Kalliope*, Penn State's undergraduate literary journal. I found the faster pace of journalism challenging, which was exacerbated by aggressive timelines and unmotivated team members. I wanted a role where I had more creative control. Book editing was more solitary, a slower process with longer schedules. So after completing my concentration in writing, I decided to complete a book publishing emphasis and pursue a book-editing position full time at a publishing house.

When I made this decision, I didn't get much feedback or assistance through the advising program at Penn State. All undergraduates were assigned an advisor, but the program was generalized and focused primarily on ensuring that students earned enough credits to graduate. There wasn't much guidance on specific career paths. To help improve my chances of landing a book publishing position, I applied for an internship in publishing and took classes that would prepare me. One of the classes required to complete the book publishing emphasis was called the Editorial Process. I enrolled, ready to absorb and apply everything I learned.

When I met the professor teaching this course, I was more eager to learn about book publishing and less eager to learn everything I didn't know about the English language. My Editorial Process class was designed to show us the standard process for how raw content becomes a book and how editors make this happen. My professor was astute, blond, pleasant and knowledgeable. Her style was business casual and her fairly straight hair curled at her shoulders. She answered questions with ease as she taught us the ins and outs of *The Chicago Manual of Style, Edition 14,* our comprehensive guide to book publishing.

One of the first editing principles that stuck out to me was how grammar rules were dictated by style (or a standardized style of writing) and that institutions of higher learning, typically run by white administrators and professors, determined which style is taught and accepted. I sometimes agreed and disagreed with this idea. It seemed to me that audiences determined style. Authorities over language standards were looking for conformity and uniformity. But what I disagreed with was the level of intrusion. Even though the primary goal was to correct without imposing your own style on the author, editors impose a style that may or may not best suit the author.

As editors in training, we were taught to edit per English grammar rules as outlined in an established style guide. For example, British English follows certain customs and American English follows certain customs even though many rules are the same. Following a style guide is standard practice for all editors. American book editors follow *The Chicago Manual of Style*, the ultimate guide for all things book publishing. Other supplemental texts include Strunk and White's *The Elements of Style*, *The Craft of Research*, and a wide range of other books editors used to guide them as they develop, check, polish and refine content. English is the language of England, so of course those that managed these style rules or writing rules were white. As an African American, I spoke English because slaveholders in America were English speakers from Great Britain—England, Scotland, Ireland, etc.

## CONFORMING TO STYLE

The language of Africans was replaced with the language of Europe. As a result, I was at odds with standardized English and conflicted about how proper my English should be.

Because slaveholders desired enslaved Africans—men, women and children—to follow their violent command in everything, everything was imposed. Enslaved Africans ate, worked, slept and spoke per the rules of the slaveholder. How we speak and write today is directly impacted by the intrusion of the King's English. The longer Africans spent in America, the less we spoke in our native tongue, and the more we spoke different variations or dialects of English. These dialects are often identified as broken English or substandard English. In academia, it's often referred to as African American English Vernacular and sometimes Ebonics. As a Black woman from Philly, the vernacular wasn't necessarily considered substandard in neighborhoods. It's just the way people spoke. People learned proper English in school and spoke however they wanted after school. I wasn't consciously aware of the oppressive nature of standardized English because outside of school, I didn't pay much attention to whether or not my English was proper. I was only consciously aware of it when I was around certain people. As an editing student, I learned about rules I didn't even know existed. The challenge was resisting the urge to break style and follow instincts based on the vernacular or local Philly slang and not standardized English. My English was being corrected, and at times it felt uncomfortable like it was some modified brand of censorship.

Learning *The Chicago Manual of Style* was necessary to be hired at a publishing house. Anything *Chicago* didn't cover would be learned on the job. One of our first lessons was on the rule of consistency. If you make a correction and that same error appears elsewhere, you must make sure corrections are made throughout. It seems like common sense, but you'd be surprised how many corrections are sometimes applied inconsistently. If a name is spelled one way in one chapter and spelled differently in another, you need to correct all occurrences, so the same spelling exists throughout the whole book. Inconsistencies are considered errors along with anything that is grammatically incorrect. Consistency also indicates style. If an editor notices that an author consistently omits the serial comma, then we know that the serial comma is not the author's preferred style. A style of writing that is consistent shouldn't be changed unless the author agrees. This is also where coaching authors comes into play—uncovering what is meant and the various interpretations between author, editor and reader.

In class, we learned the difference between proofreading and copyediting. We practiced applying copy editor marks and proofreader's marks by hand (tracked changes in Word wasn't a thing yet). We were tested on grammar rules, and we practiced writing queries to authors. It gave us a detailed perspective of what editing is like and what is expected of an editor. After taking the class, some students decided they really didn't desire to be an editor. They enjoyed creating rather than getting into the weeds, locating multiple errors, not to mention checking, rechecking and triple checking to fix not only grammatical errors and inconsistencies but the larger issues—disorganization, irrational logic, confusing sentences, unresearched content, improper tone, poor readability, lack of cohesion and flow.

Editors took much into account when editing. The better the writer, the easier the editing. Creating always sounded like the more liberating path. During classes like the Editorial Process, students really discovered which aspects of editing they mastered better than others and what came naturally. In college developing content and copyediting allowed me to use the creative parts of my brain. Proofreading was the final check, a final inspection—checking for pagination errors, cover copy, bad line breaks, formatting errors, minor misspellings or punctuation errors.

Concentration and quiet spaces mattered. Per my professor, "Shana, you will catch everything one moment and then miss a lot the next." Editing required a lot of focus and mental energy. Mastering the editorial process was a journey to standardization. The irony—I went from hating standardized testing to learning the standardization of writing, the ins and outs of convention. The upside to learning all of this was seeing the many angles of writing and the origin of style. If at any time, I wanted to break these grammatical rules or break away from style, I knew what I was breaking away from. I thought knowing the rules before breaking them was a good philosophy for approaching anything. But then again, there was an even better way of looking at it—acknowledge that the rules may not even apply to every genre or style of writing and throw myself into experimentation, which existed primarily in undergrad.

Outside of my everyday college life I didn't transform into the grammar police. I didn't edit my friends or care about their language skills. I plugged into community. As minorities on campus, we were often huddled together like we were our own college. I joined the United Soul Ensemble, Penn State's gospel choir, and we would sing at local churches and on campus. We took one trip to St. Augustine in Raleigh, North Carolina. We were so excited to gather with other Black students. The cafeteria served soul food and some of us would complain to our HBCU brothers and sisters about how boring our menu was. Our trip to North Carolina gave us a good shot of soul, strong enough to handle more of the daily whiteness of campus life.

Every Sunday after church, we would often get together in the cafeteria and talk about various racial issues—crime in the Black community, opportunities or lack thereof and racism. Sometimes the discussions stemmed from a topic shared on *BET Tonight,* a news program hosted by Tavis Smiley. We were a diverse group of Black students—African American, Haitian, Trinidadian and Jamaican. We would all share our perspectives and even our gripes with each other—debating each other on who knew their history backwards, forwards and upside down. These sessions were often a masterclass in word battling and setting up an argument wasn't a lost art—be ready to explain or disagree with facts in toe.

Meanwhile, as I continued to complete my emphasis in African American literature, my professor would lecture us on the origins of cultural art forms and folklore, gospel music and rap. One day after Lauryn Hill took home Grammys for *The Miseducation of Lauryn Hill,* some students mentioned it in class. Dr. Bell shared his perspective on rap music of that time. "This is rap," and mentioned Gil Scott-Heron's "The Revolution Will Not Be Televised." We had other lively discussions about superstition, folklorist Zora Neale Hurston, and the origins of Black art forms such as gospel music, blues and jazz in the class African American Folklore Tradition.

We continued our discussions on African American Vernacular English and its validity in the Black literary tradition and daily Black life. For the most part, as a Black child, I was taught like most children: Black English or the Vernacular was substandard and inferior. I expected Dr. Bell to have the same view as other teachers. But instead, he said the Vernacular was simply a non-standard form of English. He further explained, "To say it is inferior is to make a judgment based on a certain standard. Who said this English was broken?" My professor challenged. We were always pushed to think critically about elements of Black culture. How do we come to accept something as bad or good? In examining different forms of speaking and writing, how is one really better than the other? Essentially I adopted the same view. One is standard and the other is non-standard. There is nothing intrinsically bad about Black English.

I studied the views of various Black English scholars while taking The Vernacular Roots of African American Literature. African American English Vernacular (AAEV) vs. Ebonics—two different schools of thought surrounded Black dialect and its origins. Ebonics was based on the belief that African Americans speak a variation of English based on African language structure. African American English Vernacular is identified as a dialect of English based on European influence. The concept of Ebonics originated in Oakland, California (coined by Dr. Robert Williams) and had a focus on phonetics. The school of thought surrounding AAEV was the dominant theory on the East Coast.

It didn't really matter to me at the time who used which term. In my mind, I thought both schools of thought were correct in some way. Not loyal to either, I frequently used the term African American English Vernacular (AAEV) because that was the most common and understood term in my circles. Charles Chestnutt, Paul Lawrence Dunbar and Zora Neale Hurston wrote dialogue in Black dialect or the Vernacular. A style that was later disavowed by the founders of the Harlem Renaissance. I knew that people would understand the term AAEV much better than any other. *The Chicago Manual of Style* doesn't address these nuances, inflections and variations in sentence structure.

Style guides enforce uniformity, neat and clean. One can liken style to a seam that stretches across a hem, and the hem should be even, not uneven and without form. Style guides were an attempt to bring order to the creative arts, the language arts. But over and over, and without end, languages change over time. New words get added to the dictionary, and Black communities create, define and redefine words. As language evolves, standards evolve. A style guide keeps everything consistent and standardized, but editors reserve the right to depart from the conventions of style, keeping order and consistency but changing the rules. Capitals may become lowercase, and spelling and rules of punctuation may bend. This is especially true for Black writers who like to recreate style and question certain forms of it.

Black writing doesn't quite fit into an exact mold. It isn't British, stagnant or static. It's jazz, tippy-toed and in motion. It's an art that combines the vocabulary and form of American Standard English with the unpredictability of writing in rhythm and expressing that rhythm through new words. Editing this kind of art should follow the rules that accommodate and interpret the writer's intentions. Here the editor strives to understand each line written, not necessarily applauding how it is done, but understanding what the writer is trying to accomplish. When following the rules of the English language, sometimes they don't apply. Black people sprouted up and out of African language constructs like spyglass trees, passed through English and birthed a Vernacular rich with idioms, sayings, codes, hyperbole and new words lucid and fresh. So sometimes I would look at a piece of writing or my own writing and think—*Hmm, these rules can be bent or broken.* New rules can be created specifically for Black ways of speaking and writing in English.

In book publishing, it was customary to follow *The Chicago Manual Style* or a company's house style, but I always felt the need to modify or appropriate certain rules, because

# CONFORMING TO STYLE

I didn't see myself as someone who followed every letter of *Chicago* all the time. Standardized English couldn't be the end all be all, and every grammatical error doesn't make sense to every segment of the general population. I wanted to be flexible depending on the context or situation. Sometimes I would follow *Chicago* to the letter and sometimes I would have a more soulful approach to editing, but this was in my personal life and not in corporate America. I was never free within the confines of academia and corporate America. I wasn't savvy enough to propose a resetting of the standard—a pursuit best played in graduate school. In my editorial fantasyland, I would look beyond the basic mechanics of a sentence and pay close attention to the flow of a sentence, the feel of it. Whether it's on beat or offbeat, there's rhythm. Dialogue has rhythm, sentences have rhythm, poetry has rhythm. Editing should keep in mind the rhythm of the writer—the pace, the tone and the energy of the writing. Different styles of writing use rhythm in various ways.

Poor writing creates an offbeat rhythm. When I see long rambling sentences, I see an offbeat dance on paper, readers getting lost in a sea of misused words and jumbled thoughts. Editing a sentence should improve the flow and feel of a sentence. Reading should be smooth. It's the editor's job to match reader to author, to create a perfect union where the reader understands the text and can easily read through it without getting lost. This union or connection pulls readers into the book and keeps them there until the last page is read. Writing is a journey of knowing oneself, but as writers grow in their craft, they learn to think about their communities more and more. When writers write with only themselves in mind, they can end up with an audience of few. Those who know their readers often hold a reader's attention and gain an audience of one thousand plus.

Any complete loyalty to standardized English is a result of societal norms and expectations. We speak proper English because we are attempting to align ourselves with being American born. There was a natural conflict. As W.E.B. Du Bois suggested in *The Souls of Black Folk*, we grappled with double consciousness. There was this desire to fit into American society and a desire to shape it. The beauty of this apparent language conflict was that Black writers could choose. Since we have been immersed in standardized English for centuries, we can both master English and thrive in the Vernacular, being inspired by all that encompasses Black culture—folklore, music, symbolism, metaphor, themes and experiences.

## Beige

Steps remain progressive, quiet
Stepping rings loud, energetic
Moving yet stationary, poetic
Sand moves and flows, lifting wind
Black reveals deep growth, roots
White catches light skipping fast, scat
Warm, beige, apple peach pie, delight
Conformity becomes safety, reside

## Chapter 4

# FORM AND FASHION

### Internships and Editing Practice

With a nickname like Happy Valley, one would think the sun rays hovering over State College were extra bright, shining bold and brash like a runway model checked by no one. Penn State was known for parties, Big Ten football, the Creamery, and its large alumni association. We gained quite a reputation for recruiting top high school football players and winning major bowls—Rose Bowl, Orange Bowl, etc. In 1946 the segregated football team at the University of Miami told Penn State to leave their Black players at home. The coach responded with "We Are Penn State" and refused to play. That term would endure and become the school's most famous chant. The Nittany Lions went on to become the first team in the Cotton Bowl to play with African American players, one was Wallace Triplett from the Philadelphia suburb of Cheltenham. Triplett was the first African American to play in the NFL.

Joe Pa, college football's premiere coach, was beloved on campus, a bronze statue on display, but living and iconic. He was like the Beatles of football. Students swooned over him. From a distance he was kind and loveable like a Teddy Bear.

He was the college figure everyone loved, but I'm guessing the small Black student body merely observed this fact. We weren't too engaged with it. For us it was, go to class, get your degree and move on (with a party in between, whether sorority/fraternity led or at the only club on College Ave). There wasn't much time to get caught up in Happy Valley nostalgia.

Sports and partying weren't high on my check-off list. I hung out with roommates and suitemates. I was more of a small circle girl than a sorority girl. Since I didn't drink or smoke, I was marked by the stigma that hanging out at the library gives you—boring, studious and no-nonsense. College life was all about class, gospel choir rehearsals with United Soul Ensemble, long library stays, up-all-night study sessions and thinking about the future. Did I really want to enter the publishing field? I asked this question so many times that I decided to seize other opportunities to see if those would change my mind. I completed a minor in technical writing and considered becoming a technical writer, translator or language teacher. Since I brought my violin with me on campus, I thought about taking music performance classes or becoming a composer. I was all over the place in my thoughts.

I settled deeper into being an English major and every English major had to fulfill a language requirement. Although I already had a few years of Spanish under my belt, I chose Kiswahili. I wanted to learn an African language and the only African language offered at Penn State was Kiswahili. My professor was a Kenyan doctoral student who had a gentle yet adamant way about him. He was kind yet matter-of-fact, soft-spoken but firm in conviction. As he taught from the textbook, he would correct errors created by the white British author, a fact reminiscent of America—Black people not being in control of textbooks or other content written about them. I remember him telling us about medical groups testing on African populations and that during the early stages of birth control pill development, pharmaceutical companies tested on Kenyan women and many women and girls died.

He was also the first person to tell me about Saartjie "Sarah" Baartman of South Africa. One day, while walking through Penn State's halls, a staffer approached him. She was excited about a recent trip and mentioned she saw the bones of Saartjie "Sarah" Baartman in London. My teacher was disgusted. Bothered that someone would be excited to see the remains of a tortured Black woman who, instead of being laid to rest, was on display.

There were only a handful of people in my class. African languages were not as popular as Spanish or French, which were probably seen as more practical. Unlike Spanish, Kiswahili didn't have "lo" or "la" or feminine/masculine. Instead of "lo" and "la," descriptions revolved around "mtu" or "a person." It's context that reveals if someone is a woman or man—a fascinating fact that made Kiswahili easier for me to learn and led to my understanding of cultural norms among various ethnic groups in Africa. Learning Kiswahili drew me closer to Africa. I could close my eyes and feel the hot breeze blow through my hair, bow under my skirt and settle under my soles. My time learning Kiswahili dispelled many myths about African countries and brought an awareness of other cultural practices.

The idea that African culture did not survive slavery is definitely not true. I saw similarities between various African customs and African American cultural experiences in America. The bond between African and African American life isn't completely broken. My professor would mention African time, when people were somewhat lax in attending social events on time. *Yes*, I thought, *just like America*.

Although by the end of the class I spoke Swahili quite well, I would come to slowly forget it due to never being immersed enough to maintain fluency. I even considered studying in Mombasa to become a language teacher or a translator, but in my junior year, I saw an ad for a one-year internship at Penn State Press. They were looking for African American students interested in book publishing.

In 1998 university press publishing was overwhelmingly white, with few Black people working at university presses. An African American marketing manager spearheaded this initiative to encourage the hiring of Black editors. Even though university presses would publish African American scholars and professors, there weren't any African American editors. Diversity wasn't a high priority. The fact that African American editors brought perspectives and experiences that white editors didn't bring wasn't recognized. I applied for this internship while I considered studying abroad in Accra, Ghana, which was more probable than studying in Mombasa. I was accepted into the program after I submitted recommendations from my Kiswahili professor and two English professors. But I had so much apprehension about going overseas I turned it down. The myths surrounding Africa and my own limited knowledge served as barricades. *What happens if I get into trouble? Who would I call? Would the curriculum be too tough?* Oh, the anxiety. The internship was safe, soothing like a creamy beige latte, not too strong, yet not as delicate as a warm cup of milk. I told myself Africa was something for later in life and not for now.

I was brought in for an interview with Penn State Press after I applied. I arrived nervous but sharp, laser-focused on snagging this internship. The African American marketing manager was the first person to interview me. She was a tall, mahogany brown-skinned woman from Tuscaloosa,

Alabama—witty, compassionate, fashionable and easy to be around. It was surprising to learn we shared the same name, spelled the same and pronounced the same. That never happens. Shana is one of those names spelled several different ways with varied pronunciations. I took this awesome coincidence as a good sign. I walked away, confident that I could possibly land this internship.

Meanwhile, when I turned down the opportunity to study in Ghana, it was to the chagrin of my Kiswahili professor. Ghana represented the thrill of new experiences, untapped knowledge and unbridled adventure in the Motherland. The internship represented my career and my future life. It represented the work experience needed for employment. In contrast, Ghana represented self-discovery and a deeper African connection—an amazing journey, which couldn't be translated into anything tangible or secure at the time. If I had studied abroad in Ghana, I'm not sure I would have stayed on the book-publishing path. I think I would have gone in a different direction entirely. Whether good or bad I'll never know for sure, but I wish I could say my decision was solely based on weighing the pros and cons and not on fearing the unknown.

Shortly after interviewing with Penn State Press, I was hired. As it turned out, I was Penn State Press's first intern from the university (as I was told, interns had come from elsewhere but none came directly from the university as a part of the English department's publishing program). I served the marketing department, journals, acquisitions, and editorial. My internship pretty much solidified my path to becoming an editor. Even though I still desired a writing career of some sort, it seemed like I had a stronger future in publishing. I could envision a stable salary with benefits. When imagining myself as a writer, my visions of happy, whimsical times were laced with chasing down cash and battling writer's block or writer frustration. The journalism job option seemed regimented. Will I be able to write on command and write something meaningful without pressure? The allure of stability was strong and had the added benefit of being a part of the book publishing process.

At Penn State Press I practiced writing marketing copy and learned how to create publishing plans. Several of the senior editors on staff tested me and gave me material to edit. Everyone on staff embraced me. I felt welcome. I spent most days receiving work from various departments. I compiled and sent out direct mail promotions for the journals department. One day, Shana Foster Rivers, our marketing manager, invited me to hear Morehouse's College Glee Club sing at a local AME church. It would be my first time hearing them sing. Because there were not many Black male students on campus, it was awesome to see all those handsome Black men in one place.

They marched in, backs straight, wearing all-black suits with crisp white shirts and black bow ties. It was like watching dignitaries gather to speak. They marched down the aisles and stood at command, waiting to share their voices with the audience. You could hear a bobby pin drop; it was so quiet. We were so excited to hear them sing no one cuddled out a sound. Then, they began singing a cappella. The harmonies of this Black male chorus transfixed everyone in the sanctuary. It was like each word sung reached deep enough to lift any sad or weary heart deep in dismay. I will never forget those voices.

Seeing Morehouse reminded me of the lack of Black energy on campus and it just made me want to move on from Penn State more quickly. After finishing my internship, I considered working at a university press after I graduated. The only drawback was that the salaries for editors on the university press side of publishing were lower than average. In editorial, the starting salary then was about $20,000 per year, and there weren't any active HBCU university presses. Still, I was open to the idea and willing to make it work.

University presses also preferred and encouraged their editors to have a master's degree. This was something I was willing to do anyway, so that wasn't a big deal. I already approached several professors for recommendations for grad school. But going straight from undergrad to graduate school didn't appeal to me. I had an intense workload in undergrad. I took 19.5 credits one semester, a no-no according to one of my English professors. "You should only be taking 12 credits at a time," he would say. I was burned out academically. I also completed a minor and three out of four concentrations in the English major. Even though I took the GRE, I decided to graduate and enter the workforce. After graduating from Penn State, I applied to a few university presses but didn't land any interviews. I met a number of staff members at the AAUP (Association of American University Presses) annual conference, but those connections didn't help. Like many Black editors interested in book publishing, it wasn't the easiest field to get into, at least not in 1999.

Days leading up to my graduation, I grew tired of classes, books, reading, papers and finals. It was December 1999. I was ready to don my black robe and collect my degree. Although I felt Penn State had prepared me for the working world, I still had trouble landing a publishing position ahead of graduation. I applied for a few book-publishing jobs, but my interviews were few. I went to one interview and immediately noticed the look of surprise on the manager's face. That, "Oh, 'you're Black' face." As a 21-year-old college grad with little corporate savvy, Penn State didn't prepare me for that situation. Later, after interviewing with *Philadelphia*

SHANA N. MURPH

Penn State graduation (with my Grandmom Isabell Mosley Morrison).

*Magazine* and passing their editing test, HR told me that even though I was in the final two, neck-in-neck with another candidate, they hired the other applicant and recommended I apply for an editorial position at a wine and spirits magazine outside of the city.

When she told me the news over the phone, she emphasized how close I was to getting the job. She was almost too apologetic. Maybe she just boosting my ego, but what was interesting was that even though this magazine represented Philadelphia, a city where over 44 percent of residents are Black, they didn't prioritize hiring Black editors. Even the Penn State alum who worked as a managing editor didn't reach out. We recognized each other as I passed by her closed office.

Fortunately, the letdown from being passed over didn't hover over me long. I went back to looking elsewhere. After scanning ads in the *Philadelphia Inquirer*, I interviewed for

My bother and I at my college graduation. University Park, PA.

a media assistant position at a media planning company in Conshohocken. I accepted. Although the experience would teach me how to draft a competitive analysis report and manage a budget, it wasn't my first choice, so I stayed for a few months and left. When I think about it now, I didn't fully appreciate my media planning position. Diverse and safe, the head of the company was of color (either mixed-race Black or a light-skinned Black man), and two of the media planners were Black. As safe as it all was, I still wanted out. Looking back on it, I realize safety is not an enemy of progress but because it couldn't get me to where I wanted to be, I passed. I knew getting a position in books would plunge me into a more racially tense environment, but I didn't care. I just wanted to be aware and prepared.

But being aware of my Blackness at all times and being cognizant of how I was being perceived always felt like I was navigating lunacy. I would now enter a maze of survival tactics based on increasing the comfort of white people and proving myself worthy of white acceptance. I needed to create comfort between the interviewer and myself. As many African Americans have done, I had to learn how to disarm people so they could focus on my personality and skill set and not my deep brown skin. But certain obstacles were impossible to jump over. A racist boss was a racist boss. If a hiring manager could find a white person equal to me, she would more often than not hire him or her. Book publishers were often white on purpose. A club protecting its brand from change wanted its mission and values to remain undiluted. When a company diversifies, it may change, and many companies don't want transformation or they don't want to become a beacon for change.

If a majority white company doesn't reflect the racial makeup of the community where it resides, it's making a statement. Although they are a part of a diverse community, they are exclusive and beholden to a different ideal. They would much rather groom a white staff person to serve in the most valuable and influential roles than alter their image and purpose with a new body of ideas and perspectives. In the case of book publishing, white presses were white not because they couldn't find a Black person to perform the role they were seeking to fill. It's because white editors fit in with their corporate culture and their comfort level. For many companies, company culture is everything. When companies consider hiring Black people in an industry that is almost completely white, corporate culture is often debated.

Obtaining an editorial position at a book publisher in Philadelphia was like looking for a hoagie in a donut shop. Although I considered searching in New York, I had no connections, friends or family to help me figure out the logistics of relocating to New York or commuting. Philly was familiar, convenient and safe, but nothing moved forward.

### Talking Less

Silence isn't golden:
It's a red ink red.
Permanent and self-correcting,
It's a red bright enough to show through
the white out of endless conversation.

## Chapter 5

# COMMAS AND CONJUNCTIONS

### The Rocky Mountain Book World

The journey to landing my first book-publishing job took longer than expected, but I continued to try. In the summer of 2001, after deciding to leave my media planning assistant position to pursue a job in book publishing, I attended a Christian writer's conference just outside of Philadelphia in Dresher, Pennsylvania. As a teenager, I visited this event on and off. This time I was there to check out the various workshops and connect with Black writers. I went to enjoy myself. I wasn't focused on my desire for a publishing job at the time, but at this particular conference, I met the director of books at a small Christian book publisher in Colorado Springs. He was a middle-aged white man who served as part of the faculty.

While sitting at the same table eating lunch, he overheard me discuss my educational background. He jumped right in and spent a few minutes telling me about the company he worked for and that they had an open position. At the time, I was pretty interested, but when he told me the job was in Colorado, I smiled in disbelief. *Colorado?* I knew absolutely nothing about Colorado. Nothing. I just knew it was far, snowy and cold, with large mountains stretched beyond anyone's imagination. Oh, and that John Denver song, "Rocky mountain high, Colorado…" *Were there even any Black people in Colorado?* As hesitant as I was, I was indelibly curious. Any hesitation about moving quelled when I thought about what was missing in my life. I was not dating anyone seriously. I had no children, and I wasn't working in my field. What was the worst that could happen? If I hated it, I could just move back to Philly.

The publishing director convinced me to apply for their assistant editor position. He was quick to do so, almost too fast. I'll never know the details of his thought process. If he was interested in me as a young editor hoping to jumpstart my publishing career or more interested in showcasing my Black face as a sign of diversity and a way to shake up the company culture. At the time, my 22-year-old self didn't know much about the company, but I so desperately wanted to work in book publishing. Was I so desperate that a move to Colorado made sense? I decided to take it a step further. Not long after my meeting with the publishing director, I sent my writing sample and my resume. Afterward, the company flew me out to Colorado for the interview.

When I told my family about all this, they were very nervous about a move across country. Colorado was an unknown element. I didn't even know anyone who'd even been there. Several concerns circulated in the minds of my parents. *What if something happens to you? No one will be there. Is it safe?* To me, the only way to find answers to those questions was to fly out there and check it out.

Off I went, flying for three and a half hours. When I stepped off the plane, I noticed the wide, tan landscape dappled with mountains, and the unchipped sidewalks framed the clean roads. Colorado Springs was pristine. It had a quiet and open feel to it, vast and empty; no skyscrapers and no Black people at first glance. The air was crisp and clean. It was so sunny and radiant; the sun was blinding and shined pure white. I squinted to see the large looming mountains. They were everywhere. Colorado was picture perfect like a postcard, without stains or wrinkles, without crowds. I felt nervous and fascinated.

The company sat off a main highway with the mountains in view, of course. Again, everything was so clean. I couldn't get over how clean everything was, a striking contrast to Philly. When I arrived at my interview, which lasted all day, I met with several departments. During the tour, I saw a children's playground/adventure park, a gym, a bookstore and the executive offices. There were a lot of amenities on their campus. It was impressive and everyone seemed nice. Of course, in an attempt to make me feel more comfortable with the idea of living in such a white area, I was introduced to three Black employees. The feedback was mixed but mostly positive. Honestly, I didn't really notice anything negative or alarming during the interview or while touring the campus, so when the job was offered and the company presented a relocation package to me, I leaped forward and said yes to drastic change. Philly was moving to Colorado.

Since I'd only been out of college for about six months, I didn't have much furniture. I moved out of my parent's house and loaded everything—clothes, a new queen-size bedroom set and my small 2000 Toyota Echo—into a Mayflower moving truck. I found a small one-bedroom apartment about ten minutes from my new job. As I settled into Colorado, my new life reminded me of contrasting colors and opposites. The opposite of black was white. The opposite of hot was cold. Colorado painted a portrait of pastels and eclectic browns, swirling under rainbows and camped beneath a sun that shined clearer than crystal. Philly on the other hand dropped color on a canvas like poets dropped rhymes. Vibrant reds and sad-happy blues, clumped together like soldiers prepared for battle under partly cloudy skies. Everything that Philly was, Colorado was not, and everything that Colorado was, Philly was not. The two paintings were more than different; each displayed its own kind of beauty.

Colorado, a patched quilt of wide-open spaces and mountains, was spread out with lots of countryside. No stacked or tightly placed structures or tall buildings to marvel at or walk into. No major crowding. Colorado felt barren. It was quiet and clean and overall pleasant, but I felt invisible and small in the great wide open. I remember the first time I saw tumbleweed. While driving down Powers Boulevard, tumbleweed blew across the street, right in front of my car. Wow. The only tumbleweed Philly had was hair weave tumbling down the street—"tumble weave."

I identified myself as a big city girl, but Colorado Springs was small town living with little going on. There wasn't much noise, or sirens, or heavy traffic, or commotion of any kind. It was eerily quiet, like the silence before a hailstorm. Colorado Springs was one of God's premiere paintings. Rock formations and waterfalls, mountain peaks and plateaus, double rainbows and storybook views of nature. Neighborhoods of single homes lined up perfectly on fairly empty streets. People didn't hang out. They congregated at venues. My Philadelphia was loud, crowded and creative. People dotted the streets like lines of punctuation on paper. They moved about everywhere, hustling on corners, standing in lines, sitting on porches, socializing at stoplights, lining up at food trucks, wreaking havoc in between blocks, dancing in churches or just randomly spending time. Immersed in their art, waiting for trains, or waiting for their fortunes to change—Philadelphians were everywhere.

Violence was everywhere too—guns, fistfights and the occasional knife or skillet can be used to enact vengeance, settle a dispute or randomly hurt someone. In Philly you almost expected anything to happen because violence wrapped around many corners leaving blood and tears behind. There's no suspense, no calm, and the news reported tragedy daily. No one ever gets used to it and nothing's a surprise. But our joy becomes magnified when the good breaks through. No one experiences joy more than those who have come through fire and land on the other side with more than what they had before. In contrast, Colorado was safe. Low crime coupled with fewer people. Philly flaunted a different kind of safety—getting caught up rooting for our beloved sports teams and basking in art. Those two loves were the great escape. Artists found solace in their music, murals, poetry, ceramics, sculpture, collage, mixed media and dance. Philly had a gritty soul and Black people were plenty, a noticeable contrast to Colorado.

When I first arrived in Colorado, I only saw occasional sightings of Black people, which was usually at the mall. I was a little uneasy about it until I finally found a church to visit. As soon as I stepped in, rows of Black people congregated in the pews. Black people found! The search was over. Some Black people embraced, while others seemed distant and very much into their own clique or group. Some appeared to be indifferent to the lack of diversity and solely focused on assimilating into white cultural spaces.

At my new job, all of the co-workers in my department were white. One of them was another assistant editor like me who was hired around the same time. For both of us this was our first full-time book publishing position. My department heads and co-workers were friendly. I can't say I felt any disdain from anyone for being a Black girl from Philly. Most people were shocked that I would move out here all the way from Philly, alone, at 22-years-old. "You are so brave. I could have never done that," an editor told me.

Work was as expected. I learned more about editing and worked on marriage, teen-mentoring, and caregiving books. Other genres included youth fiction and gift books. The main

Colorado Springs, CO. My first job as an editor (assistant editor in books). I can't believe how skinny I was.

themes focused on family and community. I copyedited, proofread, checked blue lines and further honed my editing skills. My supervisors would give the assistant editors editing tests so we could see our progress. I also wrote proposals, wrote content for some titles and participated in discussions on cover design, distribution, and other aspects of publishing. I felt like a real editor. Not a wannabe or someone who just had a passion for correcting grammar. A real editor, with a workload, who was part of a workflow and part of an editorial team learning about publishing strategy, marketing and focus groups. I was learning the business of publishing and I loved that part of my job.

What I did not love was the propaganda, which paraded around the office like a gang of stealth marines. The longer I worked there, the more I heard language referencing conservative and liberal ideals. I discovered the alignment white Christians and some Black Christians had with the Republican Party. The work environment became an exercise in pandering to conservative groups and right-wing political interests. These bulletins would slide across my desk, and at first, I didn't understand why they were even being distributed. When I read them, I realized how intentional this attempt was to indoctrinate me into a conservative mindset and encourage me to oppose or support certain bills, even candidates. They opposed the hate crime bill, for example, because its protections extended into the LGBTQIA+ community. The bill protected African Americans and would make violence, such as lynching a federal crime. I surmised they weren't too concerned about Black people's safety, which historically wasn't a surprise. Some members of the KKK and other local lynch mobs were white pastors. Some white Christians, in a general sense, did not actively disassociate from these groups; there was always a weird silence regarding this.

Although I was not the most politically astute 22-year-old, Philly was democratic, not republican. I didn't have a deep awareness of any conservative element in Philly. I was automatically democratic in how I viewed politics. I grew up in it. My mom worked for democratic mayoral candidate Charles W. Bowser along with Marian Tasco and my aunt Novelette. Tasco would later serve on Philadelphia's city council and become instrumental in turning Mt. Airy's 50th Ward into one of the most powerful voting districts in Philly—aka, the Mighty 50th. I never thought much about republican or conservative agendas. Whenever these conservative bulletins would come around, each staff member had to initial in the top right corner of the document to show the distributor (or the powers that be) you read it. Sometimes I initialed without reading. I wasn't the only one that didn't like getting those bulletins. I became frustrated with the entire practice. *Is this a book publisher or a political machine? What am I participating in?*

Another thing I found insufferable was the seemingly endless portraits of slaveholding presidents on the walls, including George Washington who signed the Fugitive Slave Act of 1793 and relentlessly hunted down any of his enslaved that escaped, Ona Judge, for example. I found this admiration for the forefathers misplaced given that they claimed to be Christian. How can a Christian have zero qualms about honoring slaveholders? The portraits were posted on the walls like examples of human decency. The leadership seemed oblivious to any concept of racial sensitivity or the fight against oppression and racist systems. Whenever I commented on these observations, they seemed to understand but they weren't motivated to change. They would respond by inviting gospel singers to events and publishing a few African

American authors, but their hearts were blindly allegiant to the status quo.

They operated as if being nice to the Black people they liked, speaking in a soft voice and giving to charity made up for the fact that they turned a blind eye to racial discrimination and oppression in general. There was an air of artificial righteousness. It was a dilemma. I'm working for an organization that was indifferent toward Black people, a thorn in my side I ignored. I disconnected from reality and plunged myself into the professional demands of the day, reading through boxes of unsolicited manuscripts, copyediting books and proofreading blue lines. Happier moments were spent reading the *Boondocks* comics that I posted inside my cubicle walls and throwing paper clips at my co-workers (the occasional office play).

Pretending became second nature. I would imagine none of this affected me. I had to disconnect, reduce it all to a layer of dirt resting on me, not heavy, not permanent but resting. As if racism or complacency are easily neutralized. As if all I had to do was shake myself clean. As if all I had to do was walk outside, tilt my head up, and feel the sun's heat burn off the layers of dirt. As if all I had to do was stroll through Garden of the Gods, pass that one white rock, which stood as one of the first in a lineup of tall red rocks, pass the kissing camels, and just by mere movement feel any remaining dirt fall to the bottom of my feet. I wish it were that simple. I wish I could scuff off racism like I could scuff off dirt on sneaker soles. That dirt was the only dirt Colorado Springs seemed to have.

My work life gradually deteriorated as I felt more out of place. During this time, a book featuring multiple contributors was being written and two white conservative editors were managing the process. The book was a collection of ideas showing parents how they could use movies to teach their children. I was asked to write two chapters. I wrote on *Mr. Holland's Opus* and *Remember the Titans*. The white editors in charge of the project rewrote my content for *Remember the Titans*. They did not like how I approached or discussed race and they were't open to further discussion. I told them to please remove my name from it, which they did. *Mr. Holland's Opus* stayed in the book. The message, "we can control what you write" was received loud and clear.

As far as my social life was concerned, meeting people was challenging. But I did manage to develop friendships with co-workers. I went on hiking trips and explored the city. I walked trails at Garden of the Gods, a 480 acre park of red sandstone rock formations, and hiked Palmer Park with a co-worker and his wife. Garden of the Gods was my first hike and it ended up being one of the best ways I used to get out of my head. I liked the dirt paths, ascending and descending through brush and trees.

Coloradans are very outdoors oriented and the average local probably knew every trail backwards and forwards. Still, there was an overwhelming lack of human interaction. I didn't like crowds, but somehow I missed them. Crowds gave that feeling of being a part of something. That is what I missed—community and opportunities to connect. I missed the diversity and cultural richness of Philadelphia. I searched for anything to remind me of home. Then, one day, I saw an announcement to audition for the Colorado Mass Choir.

I had never auditioned for a choir before. Philly was a *sanging* city, so there was no need for anyone to hold auditions. Everyone knew who could sing and who couldn't. In my circles, there were so many singers that the non-singing people seemed to be in the minority. I was nervous about auditioning, so I sang the easiest song in the world—"Holy, Holy, Holy." I showed up and sang my two little verses. The audition closed with me singing with two current choir members. They wanted to be sure I could harmonize. Afterward, a week or so passed before I got my acceptance letter in the mail. I was officially in the choir. I had something else to occupy my time.

When I arrived to the first rehearsal, the choir director told us about the choir's plans to release an album. After the announcement, we were given the rehearsal schedule and the studio recording dates. LaShun Pace would sing lead for the title track, "Glad About It," which she recorded separately outside of Colorado. One day during rehearsal, we sang and modulated higher and higher toward the end of the song. I found myself outside my body, hovering over our voices. We sounded good! The sopranos were hitting the notes with precision, which for a soprano was no small feat. We kissed high notes until the choir director sensed our voices were about to give out. Gospel choir singing was a discipline, a vocal acrobatic discipline.

In Philly, we sometimes referred to high-note singing as being in the rafters. We sang songs from gospel artists and our own music written by local songwriters in the area, such as Carol Antrom. During the vamp, Hezekiah Walker songs often went higher and higher and higher into oblivion. Gospel choir singing was elevated singing. You needed to transcend to nail some of the vocal acrobatics gospel singers would do—running up and down scales and rifting in between. Hearing our voices at that rehearsal was emotional, and it's the only rehearsal I distinctly remember. We were singing Kurt Carr, which was a warm-up to practice. Singing always encouraged me. It's a communion with God. We touched hems with our voices and reached for higher in everyday life.

After we learned a list of songs, laid down every track in the studio and took photos for the album cover, it was over.

We didn't sing after that album. Not at a church, an event or anywhere. I never sang in a choir that didn't sing anywhere. Later I would hear about a smaller section of the group that sang at an engagement out of state. In Philly, my choir sang often, sometimes two days in a row. I decided not to feel like a disgruntled customer who ordered a fancy item online but received a product that barely resembled the picture. I was grateful for the high moments and pleasant choir members. This wasn't Philadelphia after all.

I appreciated the Philly choir vibe. The fun was unmatched and the joy truly was unlimited. That was my choir's name— Joy Unlimited Youth Mass Choir. The founder, who went to my church, John B. Samuel, invited me to sing on that choir in 1990. I was 13. His mother was my Sunday school teacher, and when I was six-years-old, she gave me my first diary. Journaling started with her gift. I would continue writing in journals throughout college. Joy Unlimited was really something special. We sang all over the city at large and small venues with other local choirs. We sang in competitions, appeared on television programs, and our marches down the aisles were choreographed. Our anniversary concerts were epic and began with us singing *The Lord's Prayer* a cappella. From the back of the church, we stood silent as the audience looked on and John gave us our cue. The congregation clapped and stood to their feet as we marched down the aisle. A choir favorite was *Ride on, King Jesus*:

> *Ride on, King Jesus, no man cannot hinder me.*
> *Ride on, King Jesus, ride on, no man cannot hinder me.*
> *No man cannot hinder me.*
> *Ride on, King Jesus, ride on, no man cannot hinder me.*

# COMMAS AND CONJUNCTIONS

*In that great gettin' up mornin', fare thee well, fare thee well. In that great a gettin' up mornin', fare thee well, fare thee well.*

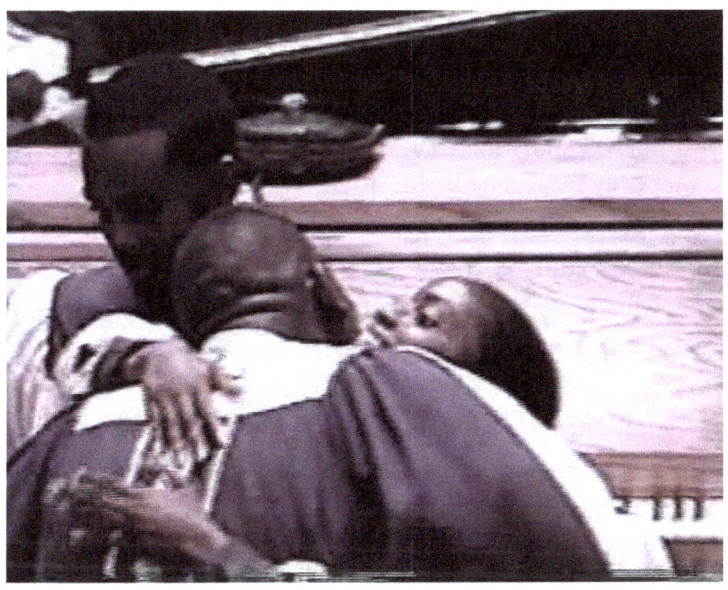

Me, my brother and my choir director John B. Samuel (founder of Joy Unlimited Youth Mass Choir) after we received a choir dedication award.

When Teddy Pendergrass invited us to sing on his last album—*A Little More Magic,* we became a part music history. What a time it was. Unforgettable.

But now I was in Colorado. I needed new adventures. After singing with Colorado Mass, interactions with human creativity and other artistic events became rare. I decided not to join a church choir. Maybe I didn't want to feel like I was comparing everything to Philly. Time for something new and fresh. I started seeing Colorado for what it was at the time—art, a canvas in and of itself, and a baseline for hearing sound in a more resonant way. Colorado was naturally acoustic. I could hear every sound, and in between the sounds, was the quiet. When sound was absent, the mind had nothing else to hold on to. No sirens, no chatter, no horns, no wheels spinning on pavement. There was nothing on the outside to process, so it caused me to process whatever was going on inside. Whatever lies beneath the normal of everyday life, the quiet will pull it up. Loneliness felt lonelier than normal. If I felt disappointed, I shed more tears. There's no escaping yourself in Colorado. There was no escaping me. I didn't even know who I was outside of Philly.

I would distract myself from how I felt by reading—Elizabeth Nunez, Edwidge Danticat, J. California Cooper, Toni Morrison, Dr. Tony Evans and others. I joined the Black Expressions Book Club, which delivered books to my first-floor apartment. Books didn't replace my need for human interaction, but they did give me an outlet. The books were the only thing separating me from becoming discouraged about both my life as an editor and my social life. I wasn't good at editing my own life to make it better. I'd rather skip pages and omit sections. Since I was away from family, I hung out with people as they had time, but I wondered if anyone could relate to my culture shock. I used to think I preferred my own company, but the more alone I was, the more I realized I needed a buffer, someone to talk to about my thoughts.

When my parents came to visit me in Colorado Springs, we went sightseeing. I was too excited to see them to share how I was feeling. I just wanted to have fun. One of the places we visited was the Manitou Cliff Dwellings museum in Manitou Springs, Colorado. These were the living quarters of the Anasazi (as told to me). We explored all the open spaces. I entered along the side of the mountain to find rooms and doorways surrounded by rock. I imagined how adults and children would roam and navigate using the ladders and window openings to go in and out. When I entered those spaces and started talking, I could hear how distinct my voice sounded. I heard myself and others differently. Voices were three-dimensional, clear and piercing like light passing through crystal. It made me want to sing. It was the perfect environment for singing or hearing music. You could hear tone and pitch with only a whisper. I could imagine an entire album being recorded there—the notes floating on thin air, bouncing against rock, and into the mics they would go. To truly hear all the dimensions of sound is grounding and lifting, a high for the artist and the listener.

After visiting, my parents were much more comfortable with me living out there when they realized how safe it was. I can't imagine a parent being too thrilled with the idea of their only daughter moving clear across the country, barely out of college and in a state no one in my family had ever visited. But the fact that it was free of significant crime relieved them. They liked Colorado, generally speaking. When they left, I returned to where I had left off in this Colorado Springs experiment.

Visiting the ancestral home of the Anasazi at the Cliff Dwellings Museum.

Entrance into the Cliff Dwellings Museum, Manitou Springs, CO.

Cliff Dwellings Museum.

## COMMAS AND CONJUNCTIONS

My mom and I at Garden of the Gods in Colorado Springs, CO.

Me and my dad in Colorado.

Posing with my mom at Seven Falls in Colorado Springs, CO.

Colorado mountains west of Denver.

In my everyday life, I didn't usually feel any palpable racial tension in the community. The Black population was small and life was uneventful. It seemed like I was too minor of a pretty brown speck against the white landscape of Colorado living to encounter racial hostility. That idea was short-lived. One day, while driving around my neighborhood, two white men in a red truck ran me off the road. Fortunately, I went into the dirt. I didn't crash or damage my car. Afterward, they laughed as they flew by. I was shaken, but I just sat there in my car for a few minutes and drove home. It was the first time I had experienced anything like that. I didn't breathe a word about it to anyone. If I told the people around me, I'd have to manage their emotions and mine. I didn't want to live in panic mode. I wanted to pretend I imagined it, and for some reason, I didn't think it would happen again—and it didn't. I subconsciously learned to avoid or instinctively not drive in certain areas or say certain things. This was in some ways the beginning of my coping with anything racist, whether that was in my daily life or my work life.

Whenever my family came to Colorado, I was more aware of my own presence. I felt alive, as opposed to feeling separated from the ins and outs of life. Usually, when I'd walk around Colorado, I was anonymous. People see you, but they don't really see you. I am a quick glance—my face unremembered. Everyone was minding his or her own business, so to speak—seeing shapes but not details, seeing a body, not a friend. I would need formal introductions, a gatekeeper to true social interaction. That is pretty much how I met people—rarely on the fly, walking through the mall, or sitting on a pew. People roamed and congregated but the atmosphere was rather neutral with not a lot happening on the surface. Most social activities occurred in people's own homes. They would invite people over or go out to eat.

One day at work a co-worker introduced me to a friend of hers. She was a young blond and a direct descendent of Charles Hires of Philadelphia, the founder of a popular brand of root beer, which the family sold to Coca-Cola in the sixties. She appeared quite normal. She didn't have that snooty, old-money feel that I expected. She spoke of her family's past-time of pulling out the family recipe and making a batch of root beer. I could picture the family gatherings. Everyone assembled in the kitchen, laughing and smelling that sweet sassafras scent. Children running around the kitchen table as parents gather glasses. We didn't have more than two conversations, which was how many interactions were in Colorado Springs—polite yet fleeting.

There were many pleasant interactions, not a lot of depth, but nothing off-putting. I thought this would be an ideal time to create and finish one of my short stories. But although the beautiful mountainous landscape and the crisp clean air brought a certain amount of serenity and peace, I didn't spend much time creating. Colorado should have inspired me, but I was so emotionally drained by what was missing that I could not focus on anything else. There was too much quiet, not enough music, not enough voices, not enough art, nothing to motivate me or get me feeling alive with purpose. In Philly, I was always creating, writing, sketching, singing or playing an instrument. I didn't release any of it, but the creativity was always there. I could always hear my poetry. In Colorado, I was roaming and discovering. It was as if I was on an expedition, but it was a different kind of journey—a segue, a sidestep.

As I was attempting to dig my heels in to develop a richer social life, it became more and more apparent that in Colorado Springs, most people were married, and the dating scene was pretty much non-existent. Much of the Black population was military and my two of my friends had military husbands. We would hang out at the local club, the only Black club I knew of in Colorado Springs—La Jazz. Or we'd gather at someone's home. Dating was a bit of a paradox. I encountered very few single Black men that dated Black women. I ended up dating men who lived in Philly, which created its own problems—long distance never works. Dating outside of my race wasn't considered. Doing so would've been like adding salt to an already salty dish. Settling into Colorado was already a challenge. It was the epitome of awkward. My social life plateaued at "sorta happy" as my work life veered off in an interesting direction.

One of the few African American co-workers I knew worked in marketing and pulled me into a new initiative. The company sought to expand its footprint in the Black community, and as is often the case, the Black community was targeted as a viable consumer base. This organization was the latest to target this untapped market. The exciting part for me was the upcoming exposure to the marketing side of books. I had some exposure to marketing at Penn State Press, but it was more introductory. This time I would learn more about planning, strategy and branding. The company hired a Black-owned company to research, present data, manage focus groups, offer strategy and help launch their Christian African American-centered books. They arrived prepped and ready, but the organization was not ready.

Executives listened to the recommendations and hosted focus groups, but they weren't genuinely committed to the plan and were more loyal to their white conservative base. In order to be fully invested, they would need to understand that they needed to appeal to the greater Black Christian population and not the few right-leaning Black Christians. Despite the company's lukewarm "buy-in" to the proposal, I pushed through one title for African American families written by a Black couple. I learned an important lesson that would come up again and again. Many white companies are looking for Black people to get on board with their ideology. They are not willing to turn their backs on anything that would disrupt their profitable foundation even if that foundation was infected with white supremacy's diseased legacy. Even though I felt empowered for a brief period of time, I grew tired of their wishy-washy stance on change.

Not too long after, I was sitting at my work computer, and my co-workers began whispering. Quickly a group gathered in a department conference room. I figured I'd get up and see what was going on. As I entered the room, I saw the gray-black smoke on T.V.—a plane just hit tower two of the World Trade Center and then D.C. I knew someone in New York, so I immediately called her, and she was fine, as was her family. I did not know anyone who died due to the mass destruction. But the extreme loss of life—first responders, workers in the World Trade Center and anyone too close to the collapsing buildings brought collective despair.

*Wow, did that just happen?* American life changed forever—airplane travel changed, New York changed, national security changed. What remained were memories and the emotional quest to rebuild and restore. The vivid memories captured through photos I took as a ten-year-old came tip-toeing back. My elementary school took my fifth grade class on a field trip to New York. We climbed up the Statue of Liberty, ate larger-than-life slices of pizza and visited the World Trade Center. I would never see the Twin Towers again or feel my ears pop as my mom and I went up the elevator. I remembered the view from the top floor and how I could still see the top of the Empire State Building through the fog. At that point, I'd been in Colorado Springs for two years and life was static. I had a love affair with nature and met people who introduced me to different ways of thinking and living, but the Colorado Springs experiment was over. I left with a card from my department which said, "Goodbye. Everyone here will miss you! From the big wheels on down … to all the loose nuts!" Eighteen people signed it. One comment read, "This place won't be the same without you."

The view of the Empire State Building from the World Trade Center in 1988 (barely seen due to foggy skies).

## COMMAS AND CONJUNCTIONS

The top floor of the World Trade Center from 1,355 ft.

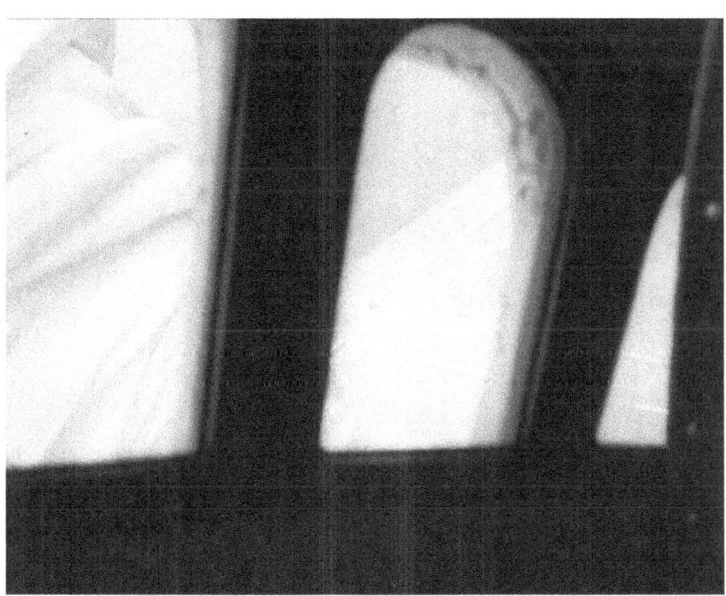

Taken from the crown of the Statue of Liberty. My mom and I walked
up the spiral staircase. It was incredibly hot that day.

### Philly

Red beads
Broken strings
Falling into rainbow puddles.
Strings of beads wade in color
before shooting up again.

## Chapter 6

# SHIFT P

### The Philly Publishing Scene

Traditional publishing in Philadelphia arguably began with William Bradford and his son Andrew in the early 1700s. They published religious texts and newspapers. Not long after, Benjamin Franklin, who learned the printing trade in Boston when he was a preteen, relocated to Philadelphia as a teenager and established a printing press that, by 1740, published the first novel printed in America—*Pamela*. In 1782, the first English bible was also printed in Philadelphia, but Boston had been well established in the printing industry, publishing various publications since 1639. Both *Our Nig* (1859), the first novel written by an African American, and the liberation narrative *The Life of Josiah Henson* (1849) were printed in Boston. Eventually, New York would come to dominate the publishing scene, but prior to that, Philadelphia was home to eighteen presses. Philly's niche was medical texts. Science publishers were a significant part of book publishing in Philadelphia. By 1800, 70,000 books were being printed in Philadelphia.

In light of this, it makes sense that I would find my next editing position at a science publisher. At the time, science and academic publishers—Elsevier, Wolters Kluwer and Taylor and Francis—dominated the book publishing and journals space. There were some smaller trade book publishers in the city, but textbooks and other academic titles represented a huge chunk of the publishing market in Philadelphia. For example, J. B. Lippincott & Company's origins trace all the way back to 1792. They published almost all of Zora Neale Hurston's books when she was alive (except for *Seraph on the Suwanee*). J. B. Lippincott published *Their Eyes Were Watching God* in 1937. Still called Lippincott to this day by locals, it eventually became Wolters Kluwer years after a merger in 1998.

When I decided to relocate back to Philadelphia, I only found openings at science or academic publishers. Since I had a minor in technical writing, medical information and technical terminology weren't foreign. I applied for a developmental editor position with one of the largest science publishers in the world. The job included some editing and project management duties like tracking the progress of a manuscript, creating a schedule, keeping authors on track, collecting signed contracts, checking art, managing the copyediting progress of freelancers, sending out grant-in-lieu-of-royalty payments, participating in marketing strategy meetings and some traveling.

The position was in Old City Philadelphia, an ideal location. Great food and excellent shopping. I always wanted to work downtown because I wanted to be in the middle of everything. Every time I stepped out for lunch, I embarked on an adventure to get to know the area, walking up and down Chestnut Street, Walnut Street, and window-shopping around Jeweler's Row and 6th street. A string of amazing restaurants, such as Jones and Buddakan were in the area, and on any given day, I would pick up some handmade shea butter body cream or grab a bite at Reading Terminal. It felt good to be home. Every morning I would hit the subway and the El to the Curtis Center, a historic statuesque building with marbled walls and floors. After orientation, I settled into my cubicle near four other development editors (or DEs as we were called). Everyone was friendly and career life was moving along just fine. I was given 10 titles to work on, each publishing at a different time of the year. My first supervisor was a blond white woman who despite her classy sharp attire was less put together in the area of professionalism. She was demanding, moody and didn't seem to have much of a role. I don't remember what she did besides supervise the DEs.

When I interviewed with her, I wore a black suit (skirt and jacket) with a white blouse and black heels. My straightened hair was pulled back and I was prepared for each question. She was impressed and quite pleasant during the interview. As soon as I was hired, she settled into her role as a stern micromanager. I remember feeling on edge and frantic, desperately getting out every email and completing every task on time and as quickly as possible so I could avoid one of her rants. She fortunately got pregnant and quit. *Glory!* My next boss was a laid-back white man whose wife was a Denver native—the irony. He was the exact opposite of my previous supervisor and never concerned himself with what the editors under him were doing. He didn't give us much direction or leadership, but he was knowledgable and kind. We would talk about Colorado from time to time.

The best thing about that job was the perks—fancy business dinners, catered marketing meetings, lunch outings, posh Christmas parties and business travel to conferences. The job itself, though, was monotonous. It drove me crazy. It was as exciting as a martini missing its two olives—the olives being the best part. The excitement happened during editorial meetings and cubicle gossip. I quickly got bored with my daily routine. There weren't any opportunities to advance or move about the company. Every day I worked with titles in the fields of cardiology, ophthalmology, endocrinology, emergency medicine, oncology, critical care and anesthesiology. Prominent physicians served two- to three-year terms on editorial boards that managed and approved content. Interaction with them was more minimal than working with nonmedical authors, because those authors were often world-class surgeons and speakers who were authorities on interpreting medical claims and relaying medical assumptions and perceived facts.

Much of the content I worked on was commentary—views on leading or hot topics from medical journal articles. These books were used to help the medical community keep up with the latest perspectives and opinions on various conditions, diseases and practices in medicine. The doctors were ultimately responsible for what was said in the book. Editors did not impose too much editing on them because we were not clinical editors with medical degrees. We were authorities on written expression and not authorities on fixing inaccuracies. Editorial boards were too busy to develop relationships as deep as what editors can form with trade authors. I was basically collecting and delivering information from their assistants—collecting chapters, managing the copyediting process, compiling feedback and presenting marketing data. The one non-office work-related task I enjoyed was the required travel.

I flew to New Orleans pre-Katrina one year to meet with my Cardiology editorial board and present sales and marketing reports to them at the American College of Cardiology Conference. The cardiologists were friendly and excited to hear about what I had to share with them. I met them individually because they all had various commitments at the conference. It was my first business trip and I traveled alone. What I loved most about the opportunity to travel was the change in scenery. I worked and went sightseeing. I walked up and down Bourbon Street and visited the French Quarter and the waterfront. I was only there for a short while, but the city made an impression, even if it was largely food related.

    Now, Philly has good food. It's inventive, hearty, old world and rich—Black, Dutch, Italian, Polish and Irish. The oldest parlor in America, Bassett's Ice Cream, resides inside Reading Terminal, and Hercules Posey, the enslaved chef of George Washington, impacted the culinary imagination long after escaping slavery in 1797. Philly was arguably the birthplace of what we call American cuisine. Modern day Philly served cheesesteaks, cheese fries, soft pretzels, strombolis, hoagies, water ice, Hires root beer, funnel cakes, Tastykakes, peanut chews and the cornerstones of soul food—cornbread, mac and cheese, fried chicken, fatback and greens, etc. There was a keen emphasis on heaviness and flavor and not so much on fresh and healthy. Soul food hummed and bopped its head more than it checked your pulse.

    We liked our food like we liked our music, neo and free, but Louisiana had Creole, red pepper, red sauces. Red. Red. Red. As a child, my family would sprinkle Louisiana hot sauce on our food but that was the extent of our experience with Creole-style cooking. We were East Coast—fast. Fresh in song only. But in New Orleans, food was a slow-cooked marvel. During my trip, I had lunch at the Marriott on the waterfront. I didn't have a list of restaurants to visit or a plan for where to eat so I just ate at the nearest place. I was alone and quickly sat down to eat so I could get to my board meetings on time. They were held in-between conference sessions. And the food—it came to me like a dream date rolled up in a blanket of clouds. As I ate, I felt lifted and grounded at the same time, treasured like a newly discovered star. I hoped my delighted stomach would feed my mind and keep me from saying anything stupid or bizarre. Because prominent doctors surrounded me there were moments of insecurity where I second guessed every bit of information I was about to share.

I met with two physician authors that day: one cardiologist, one cardiac surgeon. They were all so serious over the phone and remained so in person except for one, a prestigious cardiologist from Boston who had an equally prestigious father. He was a pleasant man with a cheery smile and straight sandy brown wispy hair, combed back and laying soft behind his ears. I went over a few sales numbers and marketing plans with him and he asked me questions. I was better prepared than I thought. When I checked out of my hotel and boarded the plane, I felt indifferent. My quick trip played like a prelude fading before the main attraction took stage. Work travel was more exciting than sitting behind a desk managing. I wanted something more creative. I returned to Philly desiring more.

My boredom and unfulfillment remained. I didn't delve back into any of the artsy stuff I enjoyed. I didn't sing, write, draw or do anything creative. I rested in a fog, a funk, and all I did was work. Sometimes editing can be quite creative if you assist the author with writing. Other editing roles are more project management oriented. Since I was working with medical content, my role was limited and heavily focused on project management. It was a non-creative editing position. The monotony drove me to seek creative stimulation elsewhere. But instead of immersing myself in writing or any other creative activity, I sought escape. I started thinking about why I was unhappy and why I couldn't just "get happy." I made decent money. I worked in my field. I had friends. I should feel grateful and blessed, but I felt stuck. Unhappiness is not really about what is happening. It is often about what isn't happening. And as a writer who had become an editor, I was outside of the creative world of writing. I had abandoned all the writing projects I started in college, and after graduation, I became a wanderer, an unbound floating piece of paper.

While floating around, I discovered the Art Sanctuary's Celebration of Black Writing, an annual event hosted through Lorene Cary's Art Sanctuary, founded in 1998. Black writers' conferences were great opportunities to find support and inspiration. I could get back into the habit of writing, work out my story ideas and get everything out of my head. I had so many unrealized book ideas. I thought the answer was to be inspired through the creative energy of Black writers. In 2001, Dr. Haki Madhubuti taught a workshop at the Celebration of Black Writing. He shared the history of Chicago-based Third World Press. I was inspired by the story of three writers uniting to publish their own works. Their organization grew into a lucrative press, the only Black-owned press I knew of that grew this large. Dr. Madhubuti told us that a successful Black press should be located in a city with a large Black population, which made perfect sense. It would be easier to gain support from your own people. Book publishing was segregated with few Black people at the helm directing business and content development.

I was fascinated by the idea of starting a publishing house, but I didn't want to be a lone wolf. I didn't know any Black editors and none of the Black writers I knew had any knowledge about the business of publishing. I needed partners. Many people are interested in writing but don't necessarily embrace the business side of publishing. Books have to sell. If they don't sell, you don't have a business. I found the workshop moving. I introduced myself and shook Dr. Madhubuti's hand after the session.

Thinking about entrepreneurship at that time was like trying to walk through a wall without superpowers. I didn't feel that I knew enough or had enough drive and motivation to do any institution building, but of course, creators are builders by nature, and I knew one day, building something of my own would be a part of my story. I struggled to get back into my creative mode even though I was back in Philly. I couldn't create. It was a weird space that felt like being in the middle of a storm. Instead of rain, soil fell inch by inch onto my head. It dripped down the length of my hair and into my space—my personal space, my creative space. I was overwhelmed with weight, no words, no poetry and no music. *What's happening? Why am I stuck? Is this my "I need to go find myself" moment?* As it turned out, this path to self-discovery wasn't well-lit. I didn't feel the sun and I couldn't see where I was going. My visions and dreams were packed in soil, and I believed that only life experience would get me out of it. There were more life lessons to learn, and I would learn some back in Colorado.

### Art and Order

As I walked through swirls of color,
I looked for green, and
searched for pastel blues.
Out of luck, I settled on a canvas
slick and dry and blank.
It stood ready, almost at command.
Quiet, then struck with mad colors.

### Chapter 7

## COLORADO TAKE TWO

### Up Bow, Down Bow

I'd never seen an aurora in person—those mysterious displays of colorful light caused by geomagnetic storms. Although Aurora, Colorado shares the same name as this solar phenomenon, they aren't often seen in southern US. I loved Aurora's clear skies nonetheless. Not as lucent as Colorado Springs though. The Denver haze added a tinge of gray to the clouds above the mile-high skyline and it was less overcast than Philly, a noticeable contrast compared to Colorado Springs. Also, the mountains weren't at the forefront. They were in the background. I couldn't see Pikes Peak, but the less-than beauty wasn't a letdown in any sense because I was happy to see skyscrapers and more brown skin dotting the streets. I explored Denver. Walking down 16th Street Mall and hearing the tone of my own soles, I missed the pluck and bounce of playing music. The click-clack of instruments and the sound of bows skipping across strings—down and up across the bridge.

I remembered the violinists I'd heard and the time I met jazz violinist Regina Carter. Her sound added much needed rhythm to my life in Colorado Springs. Before one of her concerts, I asked her to sign my two-dollar bill. She smiled and asked, "Are you sure? You might need this one day." We laughed. I don't recall what I said after, but I never planned to spend it. I wanted her signature on something unique and significant and on my small flier she wrote, "Thank you Shana, violinistically!"

I attended the concert with my co-worker and his wife. The snowstorm paved the drive white that day. Heavy snow wasn't enough to cancel the concert and her performance didn't disappoint—the skit scat notes bounced in my head for days. Hearing violins always sparked an interest in playing again and every few years I would in my personal time—just me, in my house, with my violin. I wondered if Colorado would be like that. A state I would come back to over and over again like the violin.

This time in Colorado, I lived in Aurora, and it was Denver's turn to occupy my time. I was single with no biological children but gained a godson the year prior. Born to my sister-friend, an Alabama native who still lived in Colorado, she asked me to be her son's godmom and I said yes. My twenty-something self had zero experience with children. I hadn't even babysat within my own family. A thought bubble filled with thick air held up a script. It read, "Yippee!" and "please don't ruin this child's life." Those thoughts hovered above me. Out of my element, this god-parenthood started with a mini spree at Baby Gap and a few books from the local bookstore. I loved my new godbaby; he was an energetic and bold child. At the very least I could see him more since we were now in the same state, but that idea was cut short when the family moved to Atlanta. We would end up being separated by more than distance, but the chaos of life.

Denver was smaller than Philly, but a real city, nonetheless. Colorado Springs felt like a town struggling to stand tall

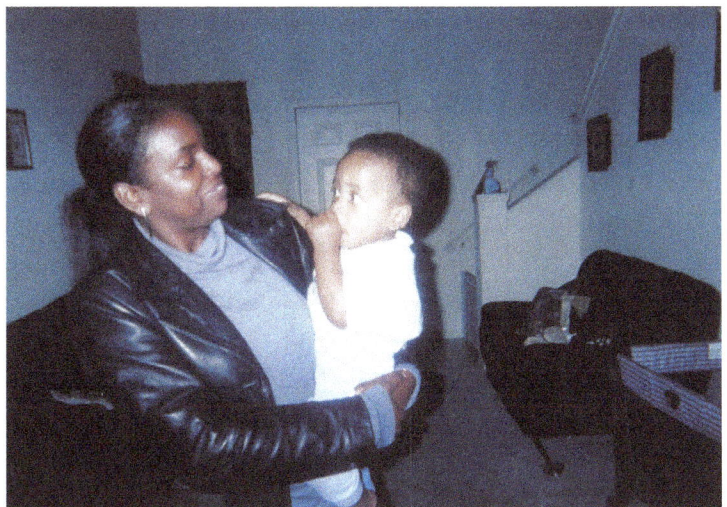

My godson when he was a baby.

enough to reach the true mark of a major city. After exploring various job openings and ripping through several interviews, I decided to take a break from book publishing. I accepted a quality assurance position in Lakewood, Colorado, working for a company that created tutorials for non-technical adults. It was my first position in e-learning. These tutorials were self-paced and designed to teach older adult populations how to use computers and computer software. My role involved copyediting, proofreading and performing functionality testing on all tutorials. Eventually, my role expanded to include working on a wide variety of documents: website copy, blogs, end-user agreements, brochure copy, captions and voice-over scripts. Coming from book publishing, it was a welcome change.

My boss was a warmhearted indigenous Hawaiian man who let me run the editorial side of quality assurance by myself. Pat Foster—he was actually brown enough to pass for Black. I had a lot of freedom there. It was my first time reporting to a man of color. When he decided I needed more staff, he trusted me to interview applicants and approve all the hiring. I began thinking about what I needed. I wanted a copy editor and a proofreader, so I created an editing test to help me hire them. Such an odd position to be in since I disliked tests and hated standardized testing. Editing tests were easy to screw up too. I both failed and passed various editing tests over the years. Sometimes I would miss the error altogether or the editing test itself was flawed—the instructions were vague, or the questions had multiple answers not factored into the test questions. I wrote a "by the book" test with definitive answers. No cloak-and-dagger. I wanted something that illustrated know-how and didn't reveal the savvy of an expert test taker. I didn't want someone who could ace a test but would fail to perform well on the job.

Once I finished writing the test, I started interviewing candidates. A particularly amusing part of the process was seeing the name of a candidate I recognized. She was leaving a company I interviewed with a while back. The person applying was the administrator of a test that according to her I failed. At the sight of her name my face turned into an Extra! Extra! plaque. She gave me a doozy of a test, which caught me by surprise because it was based on *The Gregg Reference Manual. Huh? Who is Greg?* It was an unpopular style guide that wasn't used in undergrad or by any East Coast publisher at the time, and although I had a firm grasp on proper usage and standard grammatical rules, I was out of my depth apparently.

After completing the test, she told me I failed and that I couldn't see the marked test. Who knows if I really failed it, but the interesting thing about tests is that although they are designed to measure one's knowledge of a subject, among other things, the test creator can write in all sorts of curve balls to get the "right" candidate. So if you wanted a candidate of a certain background, you made sure the test was easy for those persons and harder for the rest. Henry Louis Gates, Jr. gives an example of this in *The Signifying Monkey*. A street language test written by students was given to employees at McGraw Hill. They scored Cs and Ds. The amusing part was that she failed my test even though it was based on common standardized usage. In the end, I hired a young former newspaper editor who turned out to be a fantastic copy editor and a proofreader with no prior experience.

The freedom. I had a boss who allowed me to manage the training and supervising of my two new editors. I hadn't worked for a boss before or since that gave me so much leeway. He trusted my opinion and I didn't realize how rare of an experience it would be. Although my workload was a little heavy, I didn't run into any problems meeting deadlines or enjoying my job. My co-workers and I got along. The company was predominately white, but I was treated like any other employee. To this day, co-workers from this company would be the ones that stayed in touch with me the most. But while working there, I began longing for the book-editing life again. The book world sounded like an unrelenting sweet siren. While in the middle of editing the resource library for an SEO (search engine optimization) project, I learned about an opportunity to teach at a writer's conference.

I flew to Dallas, Texas soon after to teach on book editing at the Black Writers Reunion and Conference. The first time I went I was an attendee that mingled with writers and took workshops—one from Jewell Parker Rhodes and the other from Tananarive Due. Both phenomenal teachers and accomplished authors, their writing was like butter to me, seeping into my creative consciousness. For this gathering, I returned to teach a workshop called "Editors and Editing."

This was the first time I'd ever led a workshop. As nervous as I was, I didn't let butterflies suppress my desire to share. Since I knew so much about the topic, I used the strength of my knowledge to combat any nervous energy.

My strategy was to teach it like I was having a conversation, using handouts to help guide me. It would also keep me from rambling. It's easy to get up in front of a large crowd and get off track once you start talking. I printed a good number of booklets for my attendees. My topics included six misconceptions about editors and editing, types of editing, types of book publishers, titles and departments in publishing, how to share expectations and goals with your editor, understanding copy editor and proofreader marks, the different types of style guides and editor-writer-publisher etiquette.

I enjoyed sharing my knowledge with the Black writers that attended. I was so excited I actually talked a little too fast. I was working against the clock. Who knew how long-winded I could be once I got going? I needed extra minutes,

Hanging out with Black writers in Dallas.

but at least I shared everything on the handouts. I just wished I had more time for Q&A. My second session got more of that than the first because another session didn't follow. In hindsight that was more of a two-day class that I jammed into a day workshop. I'm glad I had a chance to present this information to Black writers who had not really been exposed to the ins and outs of publishing. The more writers knew about publishing and editing, the more successful they would be in their writing endeavors.

There's nothing like being in the company of Black creatives. It's like hearing laughter that doesn't end; it only fades and sneaks into the folds of your hands only to lift you up when you least expect it. As I became further immersed in my editing career, I didn't have much time to travel or teach workshops. Even though at that point I had seven years of experience as an editor, I knew that parts of the publishing industry were still unknown to me. I wanted to spend more time learning, so I could contribute even more.

Teaching that workshop was a good first step in helping writers become more comfortable with the idea of editing, and it's something that I would continue to shed light on, but more so as a freelancer and less in my 9 to 5. Among writers, there isn't always a huge focus on editing. Some writers think they don't need it while others find it restrictive, intrusive and obstructive. Editors may be seen as a hindrance or a blocker of creative freedom, and sometimes for good reason. Some writers have had lackluster or downright horrible experiences with editors. Some of that is because the writer and editor in question aren't clear on expectations.

It could also be due to a lack of experience on the part of the writer, the editor or both. What the writer wants the editor to do or not do isn't always clear. The writer-editor relationship is collaborative, but it only works well if both writer goals and editor goals are aligned. All editors approach editing in different ways, so it's important to take the time to talk to writers about their goals and expectations before working on a project. Now, of course, some editors just don't know how to edit and miss errors because they are inexperienced, untrained, too distracted or don't adopt a solid editorial process for their client's manuscript. There's nothing worse than having someone get a hold of your work and ruin it, especially if money exchanged hands.

No writer wants someone who will just rewrite everything or apply a heavy hand to every part of a manuscript. Retaining as much of the author's original style as possible is important. But it's fine a line, because heavy changes may be needed. When writers are signed to publishers, they're used to their work being vetted or critiqued. They may even have an MFA or a PhD. Self-published authors are sometimes caught off guard. Grammar rules and style consistency is foundational to editing, but like most things, African Americans approach every art with a certain amount of ingenuity. We reinterpret and reimagine. We challenge. But as a Black editor, it's all very subjective. Editing was an art. When I edited, I paid close attention to flow and energy—sentences that punched or flowed smooth, one after the other. My music background always wanted to insert itself into the equation. I used my ear when I read.

There were many different ways to approach editing. This was what made editing an art and not an exact science. The various approaches were based on style guides, dictionaries, author preferences and editor preferences. It's a delicate, intricate dance between everyone involved. We research, check references and keep an eye on unfounded claims, plagiarism and racist or culturally insensitive statements. Editors must serve as the ultimate checker of sorts. Some editors may choose to leave this sort of thing to the author and rely solely on the author to check their own work. But to ensure that a book is reputable, they must challenge anything that is off, wrong and flat-out confusing. Bringing order to the chaos is a part of the job.

Authors are professors, teachers, single mothers, wives, engineers, doctors, widows, seniors, ex-military, caregivers, etc. The editor role is a role that shifts and it's not unusual to bend, flex, stretch and often turn into Elastigirl. I once worked from a hospital bed answering the emails of a challenging and demanding author who wanted her book to be a top priority. Although being in the hospital made it difficult to satisfy every demand, editors in the traditional book world often worked on multiple books at a time, and I was no exception. I felt that answering those emails was key to keeping everything on track. Situations like this only added to my stress level and the realities of corporate book publishing when I was in it.

There are many writers; for example, in the self-publishing space that prefer to go it alone, which could be a disaster as well. Even if a writer masters some top-notch self-editing techniques, it's more of a cursory review that isn't as comprehensive as an editor's approach. All writers need at least a second and even a third pair of eyes to produce well-edited manuscripts. To self-publish anything without receiving some type of review is like a doctor releasing a patient from the hospital because the patient looks good to them. Patients are released after their vitals and tests are checked. There's an evaluation period. Looking good and being good are two different things.

As a writer myself, I wanted to remain free, unfettered and shielded from the slashing of the red pencil. But unchecked work is equivalent to walking around undressed or in tattered clothes. I wanted to look as good as possible, and editors did that for me. Like stylists that checked dresses for wrinkles, added Spanx to smooth away love handles, coordinated colors and patterns, and selected accessories, editors were stylists. They checked for anything that presented the writer in a poor light—errors or anything that could be wrong, confusing or embarrassing. Editors saw the run in your stocking before it passed your skirt. Editors saw the lint on your suit jacket before anyone else did.

Editors weren't wardens though; we were lifelines that saved authors from writing faux pas. That was what editors did. We made sure that between the writer and the reader, there was clarity and understanding, not confusion. As book stylists, we were writers' champions and cheerleaders; and yes, we will tell them that their first draft needs more and that punctuation was not a restricting form of literary bondage. Punctuation, in fact, brought so much color and flair to any form of writing. I loved punctuation because it gives writing rhythm—period (stop), comma (pause), dash (scat, explain or interrupt), semicolon (connecting complete thoughts), and colon (presenting lists, breaking thoughts down). Yes, punctuation was rhythm. I pretty much thought most editors loved punctuation, and as a Black editor, I used it to bring out or support an author's natural unique rhythm. This was style.

Sometimes that style was covered in ego. The ego can bury good writing under a bunch of obscure vocabulary and awkward phrasing, so much so that no one understands except the writer. Although less typical with experienced writers, editors strip that away. Editing is a strategic pull for some writers, getting them out of their heads, and into their hearts so they can write with style and spill out a form of prose that resonates and invites. No one wants to enter the mind of a lunatic. No one wants to scratch her head while reading.

Editors are the guardians of creative sanity, that is, unless the authors want to be crazy—and sometimes they do.

This renewed focus on writing and books altered my trajectory. I caught the book bug. The allure of the book world was like a curse. When I returned to Lakewood, Colorado, from the conference, I was determined to work in books again. I couldn't stop thinking about the book publishing industry. I had never worked in trade publishing and I wanted to know what that was like. So when I saw an open project editor position in the production department of a trade publisher, I applied and got the job. Off I went. I left a good job to work at a trade book publisher.

The new job was located at an organization that ran their production out of Colorado and their editorial/acquisitions offices were headquartered in New York. A few staff members were friendly and welcoming, but my supervisor was quite the character. A conniving, cold, presumptuous woman, she was the type to smile in your face and spit in your coffee. I never drank the coffee. For the first few months, I didn't have much contact with her. I avoided her passive-aggressive fury with success. The New Yorker acquisitions editors were influential like business owners that could annihilate you with any sleight of hand. Some were easygoing while others were so high society they probably called the police from their Harlem brownstones because they saw too many Black people living loud-happy.

My co-workers varied in personality—the older one, the depressed one, the upbeat, "this job will not take me down" one and the recent graduate. The office was a mix of melancholic air and dry humor. Daily we would talk about how heavy the workload was, a common thread in the tapestry of corporate book America. Every day was a new episode of post-traumatic editing syndrome. How fast can you edit a book? All the VPs wanted to know. They would test this theory too often. People were so overworked they were moody; one girl seemed to have a crying fit every day. But then again, she was already depressed. Each project editor managed multiple titles at once, and we were responsible for pretty much everything. Often, the manuscripts came in late so project editors would stay after hours to finish editing so they could forward them to the next department: art and design.

One book I worked on was *Roots*, the 30th anniversary edition. According to the publisher, they obtained the rights to publish from the family. I was excited to manage it. Even though it was a large book and I already had others on my plate, I didn't think it would be too much on my workload because I was managing the production and repackaging of a previously published title. This was, however, new territory as I learned the process for re-releasing books by deceased Black authors. During a production team meeting, staff went over which books were coming in from acquisitions and which ones were being released that year—along with other details like cost, first print-run quantity, publication date, etc. When they mentioned *Roots*, I asked for it and got it. After my boss approved, I met with her and we discussed the process and everything that needed to be done. There were no digital files from which to recreate the book and none of the acquisitions editors in New York had a hard copy, so someone randomly bought one on Amazon and sent it to me so I could get started.

I sent the hard copy from Amazon to be keyed to create a digital file in Microsoft Word, which means the vendor would type all the text into Word manually or, with the assistance of software, create a digital copy. Unfortunately, when the book was keyed, I discovered there were missing sentences and missing words. Upon closer inspection, I realized that the book from Amazon had a lot of missing text. Since I knew my dad had a hardback copy of *Roots* on his bookshelf, I called him and asked if he could send me his copy. He mailed it and I had the book rekeyed. Afterward, I sent it to a copy editor to check for minor errors. When the book was returned, I reviewed his work.

Production editors have agency and authority when it comes to the editing of a text. Whether they are white or Black, they can alter, change or remove content. For old re-released titles, it's not immediately apparent what has changed or stayed the same. Readers don't know what was added, edited or deleted unless the editor includes a note in the front matter explaining how this new, re-released text came to be. This is also true for translations. Original works that existed before computers are all in their original printed form, which means they all need to be keyed to create digital files and the oversight isn't necessarily there. Rarely did I hear of Black editors being involved with these texts, especially ones from Black authors who were not alive to oversee "changes." And to know what changes were made, a side-by-side comparison would be necessary.

Since I, a Black editor, was reading through this text I stetted (that is, reversed) any extensive changes and kept most of the grammatical changes. Every copy editor I'd ever worked with was white. In the case of *Roots*, the copy editor noted a few things that should be corrected, and I decided what changed and what stayed the same. I didn't take any of the copy editor's major changes because Alex Haley was not alive to say if something was misconstrued or if a change was correct. So I checked each change and only accepted minor grammatical changes. As the deadline inched closer and closer, I spent a weekend going through it all so I could stay on schedule. The printed pages of the manuscript created two high stacks of paper. It took two trips to even get that book into my car.

Getting this book to art and design was a lesson in putting out small fires. Acquisitions didn't have a photo of Alex Haley, so I scanned the photo on the book jacket cover and used it as a placeholder until the New York office could get a better one from the family. Using my father's copy allowed us to stay on schedule. My dad essentially saved the day because I didn't have to scramble to find a good copy of *Roots*. I gave my dad a copy of the 30th anniversary edition of *Roots* when it was released and I returned his original. When it was done, I breathed a sigh of relief.

My experience with this publisher seemed like my own interpretation of *MADtv*, only too colorful to be funny. It was like dodging the mad art of a hostile couple on set. Scene one: stand in a white room, and then run from wall to wall, avoiding flying paint. Then, scene two: a passerby stops, stares and calls the color on the walls art, unaware of anything else. Scene three: the madness, which took place moments prior, gets a frame and a name and soon, the bidding wars start as editors lay passed out alongside. Call it *Evening Editing Rendezvous,* circa 2005.

I was once given a book and told to get all rounds of copyediting completed in a little over one month. I didn't think it was possible. It usually takes 2-4 months. At least two weeks for the copy editor to edit, two weeks for me to check, and 7-10 days for back and forth shipping—to the copy editor and back to me. At the time we still mailed hard copies back and forth. I sent the manuscript out for copyediting, reviewed the freelance copy editor's work, sent it back to the author, reviewed the author's changes, and as I was close to meeting the deadline, my supervisor's manager said, "That's okay; we'll give it a few more months." All that

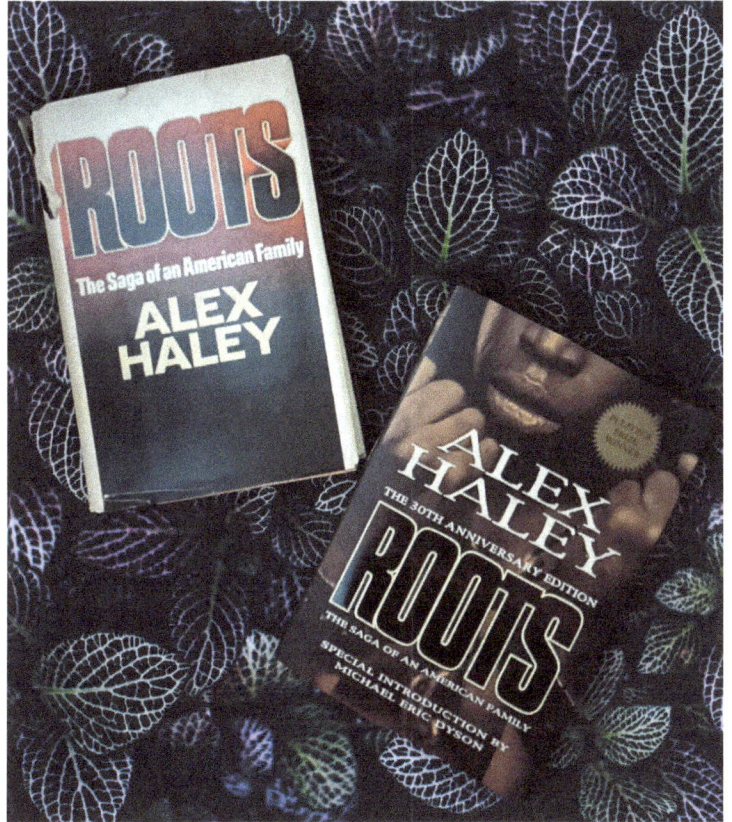

The 30th Anniversary of Roots: Before and After.

wasted energy. I think my boss's manager wanted to keep everyone on edge so he could watch us scrabble like crazy people. There was a lot of that.

The few interactions I had with my supervisor became more frequent. She became so comfortable with me that during a discussion between myself and one or two of the other editors, she blurted, "You are thinking like a Black person." I can't even recall exactly what I said in response to that, and it doesn't really matter in hindsight. It struck a chord nonetheless—like the sound an untuned violin makes when the repositioning of your finger can't make the untuned strings sound any better. That was the first time a white supervisor made that kind of statement to me, and it was said with such confidence, like she was a part of my inner clique. But in all honesty, I think she may have said it to see what I would do. The other white editors stood there in the moment. Quiet. Me—powerless.

One day I complained to a low-level white woman acquisitions editor about why another book was coming in too late. My questioning got back to my boss and a week later my supervisor pulled me into her office and put me on a 30-day probation. Her moment finally arrived. She decided to teach me a lesson. Suddenly I was in the middle of an impromptu and quite scathing performance review. This was the first time I was ever put in my place. She proceeded to list many false accusations. The accusations were not only baseless but also indicative of a greater reality. They wanted me out of there—because of a question. I guess my head wasn't down far enough and I was too brown to get away with being sassy. I was earning a new brand—difficult. I missed Lakewood where I was a valuable human being. That was over. At this publisher, I was Black, and they let me know it.

While on probation, I proceeded to do my job as I quietly went looking for another. I knew I would be taken off probation. I didn't even do anything differently during those 30 days. To be honest, I was done anyway. I didn't want to spend one more second in book hell heaven. Once they took me off probation and relayed how well I was doing, I turned in my two-week notice. I left books and found another quality assurance position just outside of Denver. I was overjoyed. I was out of there.

### Learning

Straight roads to happy are paved with light,
But going around and around stresses the heart.
Tired and anxious, the rainbows bow low,
Peace doesn't travel along a dark road.

Chapter 8

# RETURN, NEW PARAGRAPH

## Editing Outside of Books

Freedom from the corporate book world felt great, a sigh of relief. Stress brings not only uneasiness but also disease and other health challenges. My stress level when I was in books was so high, I began to feel pain in all sorts of places, mainly my right arm, which my doctor dismissed after running x-rays. I incorporated yoga into my evenings, and the stretching and controlled breathing helped quiet my body. Yoga was a lifesaver. While working in quality assurance, I decided to pick up the violin again to distract me from my unfulfilled career. I found a church home and hiked to relieve stress and exercise without it feeling like exercise. The Aurora reservoir, a lovely scenic trail, which ended at a manmade lake, had a reputation for being a good fishing area like fishing spots along Kelly Drive in Philly. My new job was closer to home, a fabulous 15-to-20-minute drive. The company even had an indoor garage inside a stately modern building off the highway.

I was back in quality assurance. The quality assurance department was similar to my position in Lakewood. I performed functionality testing, black box testing, and I edited courses for employee training, which included facilitator guides and learner guides. I tracked technical errors and checked fixes. I could have returned to my previous role in Lakewood, but I heard about a pay freeze, a hiring freeze and there were layoff rumors. I didn't want to return only to be laid off months later. The owner did end up selling the company and most of the staff was eliminated. Even though I was right to be concerned, I regretted not going down with the ship. I would have loved to spend more time with my former co-workers who I would not see again for many years. My new quality assurance team in Englewood, Colorado was easygoing and friendly. The cool thing about being an editor in quality assurance was that the vibe and pace were different. There were tight deadlines but the work wasn't as stressful or haphazard. I worked on short projects and handled five-to-ten-page documents. It was a good change of pace. In contrast, quality assurance was a cool drink in July and book publishing was dank and chilly, like a dim wine cellar (where everyone drank).

The book world seemed to attract a certain persona, a certain kind of personality. I didn't experience as much hostility, cultural insensitivity and racism anywhere else. To no surprise, publishing's history isn't clean at all. Book publishing has been around since the 1700s. An industry positioned to shape history, book publishing had a pivotal role in telling stories, managing content, suppressing content and disseminating knowledge to the world at large, including schools and universities. Whenever a Black person was placed in an influential role, such as editor, it can cause people to react defensively. Racists brand themselves as progressive and cooperative until someone comes along and represents change or new ideas. Then the truth comes out. Racists that lead departments and corporations sometimes only welcome African American staff if they know they can control them, the outcome, and control or limit their impact.

Navigating limitations was tricky. I didn't want to think about the many ways I had to get around them. But at least my new job gave me some reprieve. As for my social life—it was a bit of a hit-and-miss. I had a crew of friends who served as my cushion of air. We would hang out at each other's houses, go to concerts, and one time we rode up to Steamboat Springs, Colorado to ski. One of my friends, who I met at a singles event at my church, had a time-share and she was able to get a multi-bedroom unit for us to stay in; there were nine of us. We took two or three cars and piled in. Avid skiers, novice skiers, one experienced snowboarder and the non-skiing onlookers gathered for fun in the snow. I got away from the editing world to be social and maybe ski. We did the usual weekend getaway activities—soaked in the hot tub, cooked, ate at the table, gathered around the TV and, of course, hit the slopes.

Although I intended to ski, I decided that all I really wanted to do was relax and let my mind go numb. Getting on the slopes represented one more thing to worry about. I didn't want to do anything. I didn't want to brace myself for the anxiety surrounding reliving my childhood ski days. I wanted to relax. The last time I skied I was in high school—went to Spring Mountain, the unremarkable slopes of the Poconos, where ice and ratchet equipment abounded. One time I almost fell off the lift. While seated with the safety bar high, my feet dangled and my heartbeat felt heated and hurried. The seat felt slippery as my hands gripped the bar. We inched higher and higher. I got off relieved. I survived. After getting off and heading to the beginner slope, the falls were almost every 30 seconds, mainly because I didn't know how to manage my speed. I could stay on my skis, but my speed couldn't be controlled. I would make myself fall to avoid going too fast. Skis flew as my body went up—down—up—down like a cartoon character.

During one pass, I almost ran into a white van. Not sure why it was there to begin with. At least it was a van and not a person (as if that's better) because the first time I ever skied was at a newer resort called Blue Mountain in the Poconos. I was about twelve years old and had even taken ski lessons. I and other middle schoolers listened to the instructors as they showed us how to maneuver on our skis. It went so well that I thought I could conquer any mountain. Confident, I put on my hard ski boots, walked like Frankenstein to my skis, and made my way to the slopes. The path to the slope unfortunately began with me skiing into people. I didn't knock them over, thank God. They mostly felt sorry for me. Later, I couldn't get too far down the slopes before giving up. My brother checked on me as he flew down on his way to the lift. But after saying I was okay, I gathered my skis and went back to the resort. The walk took forever. As my bangs iced, snow frost formed underneath my beanie. I was defeated but thought I would try again at some point. My brother was such a good skier at 13; I thought it was in my genes.

Although Steamboat Springs entered my life as an adult, my childhood memories weren't that far from my consciousness. They still broke through the allure of this branded, world-renowned, Colorado snow—high class and light—a powdery soft snow that whispered in your ear as the wind blew. A snow whose sunlit flakes fell sharp on the slopes and left a glistening pop of color. In all its brilliance it said, "Come, let's ride. Be with us." But as seductive as the Colorado snow was, I stood unwavering in my decision to stay in, especially since two of us had already decided not to ski. Neither of them had skied before. Most went out to ski, snowboard or try to ski. I was more interested in just being around people. Skiing was solitary, one more solitary activity to master on my own. Solo acts were too much the norm—editing is solo, reading is solo, writing is solo and art is often done alone—I wanted human presence. Even the feeling of people around me was better than struggling through something by myself. Dealing with people was sometimes easier because I was harder on myself than my friends were and people were less demanding and not as attentive.

After 10 years in, being an editor turned me into someone unsatisfied with life—I wasn't accomplishing enough; I wasn't speaking up enough; I wasn't dating enough; I wasn't reading enough; I didn't say the right thing; I missed too many errors on a project; I wasn't good enough, etc. Not only was I correcting the mistakes of others, but my own mistakes—the "perceived" mistakes of my life. A sort of toxic perfectionism brewed a tea of discontent in my soul and I drank it often. The art of editing wasn't imitating life; it was tormenting life by feeding into my insecurities. I wasn't

Taken from the rooftop of a Parade of Homes house tour in Denver.

consciously aware of it then, and I wasn't vulnerable enough nor around enough people to gain perspective. As for skiing, maybe I would actually ski again one day, but at that time in my life, it wasn't what I valued most. I didn't think my "no" was final, but I haven't come close to skiing again since.

But even though skiing moved out of the picture, I did try something new. On a Saturday, I took a trip west. After a two-hour drive, I was at the river's edge. I could barely hear the sound of crashing waves. The gravel-packed dirt path leading to my first white water rafting adventure ushered me to the softer side of the Arkansas River. The only sounds heard were the gentle swish of distant rapids, my feet pushing pebbles into the water and the steps of our guide walking toward us. It was late August and I went to River Runners Colorado in Buena Vista with two friends.

After introducing himself, our guide gave us a pep talk on what to expect, how to paddle, and how to conduct yourself on the raft. A young bonafide white water rafting expert, he was in his early twenties and from Milwaukee. He rattled off safety precautions like he'd been doing this for fifty years. Likable, his long, semi-matted, hippy hair gave him a "I'm too cool for this river" vibe.

I was relieved to find out he was experienced, but when he gave us his play-by-play plan for "if the raft overturns," my nerves perked up. *Overturns?* The "make your way to shore" directions were a wake up call. Even though this wasn't April or May where overturned rafts happened, it was still possible for the unexpected to happen in August.

"Has anyone been rafting before?" he asked. Only one of my friends had. I was a Philly girl. We don't live near raging rivers, just raging traffic, and although I knew how to swim, I was not too keen on the idea of swimming to shore. Sensing my apprehension, our guide placed me near him on the raft.

I was seated on his left in front of him and my two friends were farther up on the right side. This positioning allowed him to grab my vest to keep me from falling overboard—just in case.

As we began sailing down the river, the first ten minutes was a pleasant ride. *How nice.* But the farther we went, the more the waters turned white and crashed against us. Our raft moved swiftly side to side, in sync with the tide. We stayed afloat but dipped into the water. Waves reached our chins and our guide grabbed my vest. We paddled and came out of the water in majestic fashion. As a group, we continued to sail through rough and gentle waves until the end of our adventure. Sliding into the river's edge, I felt accomplished. We walked away like a team of bandits from Ocean's Eleven. We took that river and left nothing behind.

Those times with friends, where I could laugh and forget, were joyful moments. With each passing day, I began missing some key comforts of home and my job became increasingly boring every day. As for my violin lessons, the first violin teacher I found to help me get back into shape was a violist/violinist like my high school violin teacher. I found her in the American Viola Society directory where my old teacher was a member. She was a tad expensive because she had played with the New York Philharmonic. I had several lessons with her, but I missed two due to being sick and she was pretty unforgiving about it. She accused me of not being serious. I didn't give her any goals, so I don't know what "plans" she had for me, but we definitely weren't on the same page.

I left her and found an equally competent violin teacher that was less high-strung and more reasonable. She gave me a piece to practice on and after a few months, she proposed that I audition for the Aurora Orchestra. By then I realized I didn't want to play classical music anymore, and I decided to discontinue my lessons. I still practiced on a regular basis, but eventually, I stopped that too. The thrill gone, I practiced with no goal in mind and no direction. It became something to do. I would enjoy the violin sounds of other players instead and retire from practice. Meanwhile, I looked for anything to fill the time and stop myself from thinking about how unimpressive my professional life was becoming. My job was a big part of my life and my social life was up and down.

Even though I enjoyed my time in quality assurance (QA) minus the boredom, it seemed that my fate lied in publishing. In 2009 the recession hit, and I was laid off from my comfortable editing/testing role in QA. I should have been more grateful for that job. It was a pleasant environment— low stress, amicable inner corporate relations and reasonable co-workers. Since I was one of the last people hired in my department, I was let go along with another recent hire. After the layoff, I was out of work for nine months and temped around the city. Interview after interview, I couldn't find permanent work. I once applied for an editing position at Janus, an investment firm located in a swanky part of Denver, Cherry Creek. The position was legal editor. Even though I was not an attorney nor a paralegal, the job didn't require legal expertise.

It was a quick nosedive after the editing test. Again, tests. This one was full of ambiguous questions and nothing law related. There were a lot of "it depends" questions. Meaning, there were multiple answers to a question depending on context or how you're looking at it. Afterward, I inquired about my test results to no avail. I could tell an editor hadn't written it. If an editor had created that test, the questions would have been more straightforward. Editing is an art and rules change. It can be difficult to keep up sometimes. Add in the Vernacular and you've got an epic word dance waiting to pop

RETURN, NEW PARAGRAPH

off. I'll tell you what, if you put a bunch of book editors together to discuss a rule from *Chicago*, they could find several different ways to correct or interpret a sentence. We could even get into a petty fight over a comma. So yeah, there's a huge benefit to having an editor write an editing test. Shortly after this, Janus laid off many positions, including that one.

Then, I edited for a travel guide agency as a copy editor, which was a nice change of pace, but it only lasted a few weeks. Eager to find my next gig, I saw an open position at a Christian publisher in Colorado Springs. I was hesitant to apply because they had a horrible reputation. A positive opinion from a someone I knew led me to start the application process and accept an editing position there. This company published books and curriculum, and I worked on the curriculum side, specifically, curriculum for Black churches.

As it turned out, the organization was grossly unstable. In the short time I worked there I had three white woman supervisors, each progressively worse than the last. It was hard to understand how any of them secured those positions in the first place, but at least the first one, the one who hired me, was nice for a time. Working in the curriculum department gave me more creative control. I could write original content. I wrote articles, activities and helped revitalize and rebrand their teacher and student materials. I even held a focus group at a local Black church. I didn't care for the one-hour drive from Aurora to Colorado Springs, but I was happy this position allowed for more creativity.

The church music, which went along with the children's curriculum, catered to white churches more so than Black churches. A white songwriter was hired to write music for both Black churches and white churches, and he received royalties from the sale of both curriculums. Black musicians and writers weren't recruited to write music for Black children. I had heard Black churches would discard the music included with the curriculum and use their own music, something white churches never needed to do. Everything centered on the white churches. I was bothered by the lack of care for each audience. People were oblivious and didn't care that they were.

One morning I was in an editorial meeting and my team was discussing teaching materials—posters, charts and games teachers would use in their Sunday school classes. They were packaged with teacher and student guides. This particular packet included a Black history piece on Dr. Mary McLeod Bethune, educator, founder of Bethune-Cookman University, advisor to Franklin D. Roosevelt, and the subject of my fourth-grade writing project titled *Famous Black American: Dr. Mary McLeod Bethune*. My co-workers suddenly began discussing her appearance in the photo. They laughed and whispered to each other about it, making fun of her. My supervisor overheard but didn't add anything constructive.

It was a teachable moment. I could have redirected the conversation or mentioned Dr. McLeod Bethune's achievements but the weight of the moment gave me cottonmouth. At this point in my life, being the only Black person in the room raised my temperature. My heart beat faster and the spotlight spiked my blood, tightened my throat and sucked my mouth dry. The irony of the fact that Dr. McLeod Bethune championed integration and racial diplomacy wasn't missed. It was not like they were snickering about a militant figure. They were commenting on an ally in the area of race relations. But if my co-workers didn't respect Black people in their everyday lives, why would they hold Dr. McLeod in high esteem? Some think of racism as operating solely as a harsh sword-like weapon, but this form is quiet and light and

### RETURN, NEW PARAGRAPH

Mary McLeod Bethune: Famous Black American

airy like poisonous gas. It lies dormant in soccer moms and church organists.

"It's a joke." That's probably what they would have said if I had opened my mouth about it. Clearly, they were having fun with it. They had no awareness. Why would they? Just as racism was learned behavior, so was respect. If white parents don't actively show and tell their children what non-racist or empathetic behavior looks like, their children may become racist by default. I'd often hear parents say, "I never taught my children to hate Black people." But the absence of direction allows hate or disrespect to grow. Everything has to be taught, love too. I wondered about the other white people in the organization. The progressive "I'll even marry a Black man" ones. How are they handling racists? Are they duking it out with them behind closed doors or pretending to be mad in public, putting on a show for Black people while laughing with their racist friends at Sunday dinner, supporting them and making their lives comfortable?

As time went on, other issues and microaggressions became a thing. No one called me the "N" word or slapped me in my face. But there were insidious stares—the kind of behavior that gets under your skin and into your joints and settles there, bringing tension, stress, headache and anger to the surface. The Michelle Obama calendar hanging in my cubicle even shifted the atmosphere. Co-workers would stop by and compliment it as if they were forcing themselves to eat at a restaurant with several unresolved health violations. On other days people avoided me or gave me incorrect information about company policies. I sat in silence during meetings. Being quiet seemed like the best strategy, but that didn't last long.

Outside of meetings, I became more outspoken. I had two new superiors on my plate at this point. Both were white women from Middle America. I had discovered racist content in some of the curriculum I was reviewing—a disturbing piece on the "Christian experience" of happy Black slaves. *Gag.* I attempted to hold candid conversations with my supervisor and her boss, who were pretty oblivious to racism, racial bias and the offensive content that should be eliminated from their Christian curriculum and publications. When she asked to learn more, I emailed her a few articles on racism and how it permeates institutions of learning, literature and curriculum. She most likely didn't read them.

Later, I asked my supervisor about considering Black children during their business development meetings. White

## RETURN, NEW PARAGRAPH

children were always the focus. African American children were not at the forefront of those discussions, even though Black churches were their customers. One main example was a proposal for a new illustrated bible for children, which contained no Black characters or brown-skinned people. Everyone in the bible was fair. My comments regarding this were ignored, and I sensed that asking questions was a problem, even when dipped in sugar. The constant pressure in the Black community to comment in a certain way—don't sound angry, don't have an attitude, watch your tone—is well-practiced. Being nice or quiet or nonchalant about things proved to be no more than a holey shield.

I spent most days writing articles and fortunately, I could replace some of the racist content I found. But I had this nagging need for resolution or something—*Oy vey*. I ended up reporting everything I was experiencing to HR. At the time, I thought I had a fairly good rapport with the HR staff. I actually thought this would make a difference. I had several rather positive chit-chats with the HR director and I thought it would be a safe place to share my frustrations. *Naive.* I'd never reported anything before. After I shared all the incidents, I was told there would be an investigation. They would assess the racial sensitivity of the staff and investigate, or so they said. I'm not quite sure what I expected. Maybe I hoped that these people, these people who collected Black dollars and smiled those heavenly smiles during corporate prayer would care enough to resolve these issues. I was naive in thinking that HR would do anything about it. I never saw any paperwork or proof that an investigation ever happened. As a matter of fact, a week or two after I reported the incident, HR told me they didn't find anything.

Shortly after the "investigation," my supervisor and her boss wrote me up. They drew up a list of allegations and submitted them to HR. When HR called me down to their office and read everything, I was angry, but unfortunately, I had been in this position before at my old book-publishing job. *Was this a pattern with me or what?* This time there was a new list of allegations. The first: I didn't tell my boss I was going on vacation. The second: I attempted to steal a laptop, and third: I didn't participate in meetings. It was ridiculous. I defended myself against the lies by sending HR the email I sent my boss about my vacation. Other co-workers never even asked for vacation approval. They just put their vacation dates on the calendar and went. But HR wasn't really looking for an explanation. They just wanted me to shut up. They wanted compliance.

I was one of only two Black people who worked there and the only writer/editor. I doubt they had ever been challenged before. In every job I held before and after this one, I was the only Black editor. Since Colorado was a majority white state (4% Black) some of the Black people were very amenable to assimilating or wanting to escape their Blackness. But my Blackness was inescapable. HR told me I had to meet with my supervisors and basically do whatever they said, or I would be fired. I was put on a 30-day probation.

I was too afraid to walk out. I truly thought my life would crumble without a job. I was in Colorado with little professional support and community, so I met with my supervisors. The two of them sat there like Shawshank wardens. They commanded I participate in meetings and I was not to tell them that Black children weren't treated the same as white children. Feeling the weight of fear, I did it. Fear will make you do a lot of things you shouldn't do. I kept my mouth shut, I did my job, and I spoke up in meetings. My bosses were pleased, and I was given a favorable review. One or two weeks later, I was laid off after I received positive feedback from my supervisors. Interestingly enough, one week prior, I was told my product line saw an increase in sales due to the new content and branding guidance I provided. *Humph.* I told myself: *You should have just walked out.* I would have been out of a job anyway. If I could have edited this part of my life, I would have slashed it to death with a red pencil. Or better yet, I'd revise it, recreate it in a daydream. I would rewrite it:

> *When I think about it today, I'm glad I quit. I didn't fear losing my job. Even though I thought my life would crumble, I found work and sued that company, settling out of court. After the court case, the company committed to hiring more Black editors and improving their representation of Black children in their books and curriculum. Black children and white children were now equally embraced. I did not succumb to fear. Bravery prevailed and change flew in like birds of prey attacking anything dark and unjust. I felt lighter and higher. I opened my mouth and the earth moved in my favor. My new job was a top position with better pay, a large office and an assistant. All hail, this Black editor's time had come.*

But there are no rewrites in life, just future drafts. All I had was my belief in revision or taking another stab at it—to reframe my thinking for the future. I can learn and move forward. My soul sang an old gospel song from my choir days, "*I will run on. I will run on, just to see what the end will be, just to see what the end will be. Oh, run on.*"

Soon after, the stresses of corporate Colorado life softened some. Before my layoff, I grew tired of renting and bought my first home, a new two-story condo with stucco exterior and stone walls, a fireplace, a loft, an upstairs laundry room, a master bath and a larger-than-I'd-ever-seen-in-Philly walk-in closet. I didn't grow up seeing a master bath, but now I had one—with a soaking tub, no less. Large windows let in so much light I thought the hereafter was near. It was bright, shiny and mine. This seemed like good living despite my dreadful corporate situation. My mom flew down for the closing, and she loved my new house. I sometimes wondered if buying it was a good idea. Living in Colorado didn't feel permanent, but maybe subconsciously, I wanted it to be. I enjoyed the quiet, but not the disconnected feel. I missed the Black community. Black people lived in Aurora, but there wasn't much community. No community and a dreary workplace—not a recipe for social or professional success.

 I traveled back and forth to Philly during the holidays and family would visit. My big brother visited me one spring. I didn't tell him much about my work issues. I didn't want to think about it. My life, a blend of secret disgust and high-life adventure. Colorado, an up-bow/down-bow journey. Happy to have family around; we explored parts of Denver I hadn't been to yet. We went to Elitch Gardens Theme and Water Park and took on the roller coasters. We rode one roller coaster and decided one was enough. It was the last time we would ride roller coasters together. We used to ride every roller coaster out there. Our footprints were all over Jersey's Great Adventure and Pennsylvania's Dorney Park. But now we had evolved. Life was a series of growth spurts, and after each one, I realized there was something new to explore. This was one of those times. And as quickly as it came, the weekend was over, my brother returned to Philly, and Monday took me back to my everyday reality.

 After being laid off, I landed another job as a writer/editor in the communications department of a nonprofit.

**RETURN, NEW PARAGRAPH**

Family visit. Meeting my brother at the Denver International Airport.

And to my surprise, I now saw more than one or two Black people. Even though I could still count them on one hand, it felt like I was swimming in a melanin river. That's how it felt being in a white under evolved environment, like I'd just come out of the Sahara. Now, days consisted of lunch with Black co-workers and Black-central conversations at the office. I felt a little freer, but the Black staff and I were caught up in a system of hidden agendas, elitist thinking and emboldened sexism.

## Bending

See women run
Run through fire
See women step
Back and forth toward power
See women dance
behind whitened windows
See women bow in
Stamped small spaces

## Chapter 9

# COLON

### Interpreting Self

Statements. They seem definitive. When you say something, the words appear final and cemented in time by those who've heard them. But life is an accumulation of statements that can be followed by periods, dashes, commas, semicolons or colons, and even erased. There's always more to say. My new position was in Colorado Springs. I continued to commute to the Springs from Aurora, getting up at 5:30 in the morning to get to Colorado Springs by 7:30—home by 4:30 pm. After a quick and pleasant interview, I was hired before I could blink three times. Since I was abruptly laid off, I didn't have time to consider my options. This *was* the option, and I went with it, but the transition felt awkward. Every day I drove into the parking lot feeling like I was driving back in time. Although I was born in the late 70s, I felt eerily older. Like I was moving through a black-and-white film—some parts were silent while others flickered with sound. Color was outside the four walls and inside the atmosphere was square like old PC monitors, the workflow, unrefined, without tempo or versatility. Not enough salt to preserve my joy and too much stale sugar. In fact, two of the missing ingredients were perspective and sincerity. I would explore and notice clothing styles (most dressed basic), and some people spoke like they were unaware of what was happening in the world— cut off from knowledge and ill-acquainted with differing opinions. Red rock and landscaped gardens surrounded the office building and wildlife encroached from time to time. One day our facilities manager gathered us around a large steel drum and gave us a cautionary tale about rattle snakes in the area.

Now by this point I had grown to like hiking. I hiked Royal Arch in Boulder and explored the Aurora Reservoir, so I was especially concerned. He proceeded to pull a rattle snake out of a barrel drum and said, "Be on the lookout for rattle snakes. Most people get bit because they don't see them and after stepping on them, they get bit. If that happens to you, forget about what you saw in the movies. Don't try to suck out the venom. Just call 911. The ambulances come stocked with treatment. They'll come to where you are, give you what you need onsite, and send you off." We all stood rather stoic and afterward it was business as usual.

Outside our building the gardens and architecture resembled the estate of nobility with its castle structures and contained fields—a peaceful energy. Inside headquarters, I was much more on edge. I frequently got into conversations with co-workers who didn't understand the crescendo and decrescendo of single life. It was frustrating being in an environment where so many were long-time married and the mere mention of my single status led people to think I needed to hear encouragement rather than words of acceptance. I was a single woman surrounded by people who couldn't always relate. In that place, singleness was a dark scabby brand. Some co-workers looked at me with sad eyes or they didn't look at me at all. *Something must be wrong with her if she's still single.*

Walking up to the Royal Arch in Boulder, CO. I discovered this trail through a hiking book a friend gave me. I chose this particular hike because it was said to be an intermediate hike. Definitely a misprint. It was a tough trail. LOL.

The view from the Royal Arch trail in Boulder. I got to the top exhausted but the view was worth it.

I was childless, unmarried, a descendant of enslaved African Americans, and an educated, opinionated thinker who had a reputation for challenging convention (as Gen Xers often do). As I was—I didn't think many knew what to do with that. I felt like an oddball who knew how to write and edit, compose and challenge. But I didn't know how to get what I wanted. I didn't know how to connect with the right people and flourish as a creative. The goal was to be nice to everyone and suppress myself as much as possible within the corporate space. I wanted to stand up for my Black self, my woman self, and my buried self. But was I clear on who I was and what I wanted?

For sure, I focused too much on how I was perceived and didn't spend enough time being clear on what I thought, being brave enough to stand on my convictions even if it meant losing a job. But it could have been worse. I wasn't inducted fully into any of the organization's inner circles because I was a new employee and unmarried. "My life wasn't legit, until I got married," was my take. So any scandals involving staff never came near me because I wasn't as indoctrinated. Everything happened among married leaders. They were at the forefront. I was the fly on the wall. It was my protection—singleness equated to safety in this case.

Although I wasn't desperate to hook up with just any man, I was aching for companionship. Whether that was platonic or romantic, I didn't care, as long as it was consistent and reliable like the Colorado sky at 7 am. I wanted marriage but what type of marriage, what type of man? When who you are is in flux, it's hard to attract the right partner. Existing in this black-and-white workplace was mostly work, but I did get to play. Yes, some co-workers didn't know how to engage with me—encourage me, give me advice or play matchmaker—but early in the morning, I would have these great stress-relieving convos with my cubicle mate who was white, married, older and amiable. She and I would arrive at the same time, and we'd have candid conversations about everything from health to movies to family to word games. We laughed like free people. But every day, it was all interrupted by the corporate schedule.

I would frequently find ways to take breaks in between interviewing staff and writing articles for the company's website and the annual report. I was finally interacting with more Black people than usual, so I'd wander into their departments when they had free time. With more of them around, I felt less concerned about how I would be treated; two Black men were on the executive leadership team. Black conversations were empowering and took the edge off of working in black-and-white. One of my Black co-workers was across the hall in a different department and we often went out to lunch. Those times were vivid. We'd get together and talk about our lives as Black women in the Springs, family life, company drama and weekend plans.

The company held annual conferences and I flew to one in Louisville, Kentucky. It was here and in similar forums that I would come to understand their position as supporters of a white male headship structure in and outside of the church, in and outside of marriage. It was like many white women were the supportive veins and the assistants. They weren't the visionaries; they were the hanging vines. I honestly didn't feel much of that in the Black American community. Black women were celebrated more, and we led more, but the tenants of organized religion did complicate everything and skewed some interpretations of scriptures. During this time, I became more intentional about my own spirituality. As it happened, my pastor at the time taught hermeneutics, exegesis and homiletics at my church. I wanted to explore the dynamics of belief and the nuances of interpretation.

In college, I was in a similar position. I interpreted and studied texts—Black texts. This time I'd explore this in my spiritual life. Why did I believe certain things to be true? How did I interpret certain events in my life? What does it all mean? How am I defining it all? I felt impelled to do my own soul work, as some would put it. I fell back into this idea of interpretation and meaning, which I had been engaged in throughout my life. I signed up and my church class's first assignment was to choose a passage of scripture, roughly 8-10 verses that you did not understand and wrestle with it, interpret it, understand it and break down the reasons behind what you think it means, what others think it means and what your conclusion would be.

We used a variety of interpretive tools, different expository dictionaries and texts from various theologians. I explored liberation theology, systematic theology and womanism. Instead of exploring literary theory and interpreting African American literature like college life, I was interpreting my own Black life, my thoughts and experiences and how that all coincided with what I believed to be true. My mind and nobody else's was the subject. I examined how scripture and biblical teaching influenced me. I chose a section of the Bible often used to enforce sexist ideals. 1 Corinthians 14, where Paul told women to be silent—a point that had been exploited in the name of spiritual order and social decency. As written, men are allowed to lead conversations in church and women should be tight lipped. Growing up, I'd heard very literal and expansive interpretations of this, which turned into "women shouldn't preach sermons in front of men" or lead general worship. I realized these views were subconsciously repeated in my head and remixed into blues songs that showed up in my life as swatches of color switching out during various phases of life-changing channels—red for anger, black for discovery, white for realization, gray for doubt, gold for triumph and blue for challenge.

Learning about words and historical content led me to interpret 1 Corinthians 14 in a liberating way. I didn't conclude that women were at all the focus of those Corinthian verses; Paul spoke on order, not control, and even more succinctly, he addressed the disorder occurring within this particular church during this particular time. This passage and others explored the solving of a problem rather than controlling the status of women. This was an important realization because I discovered just how much I internalized something skewed to lower me. What I had heard growing up, whenever these scriptures were taught, was that women couldn't do this; women shouldn't do that—because the Bible says. It latched on to me and whispered—*women are less than, you are less than, women are bound and you are bound*. I didn't feel free in church back then. Those thoughts buried me as a teenager. But as an adult, after examining it all for myself, there were now cracks in the soil of my life.

Church leaders never degraded women or spoke harshly. Everything moved soft, no vitriol, just a matter-of-fact "this is how it is." Women could teach children and other women but not mixed crowds, and women couldn't speak during communion services. Growing up I was told women could sing in the choir and play instruments, but they couldn't lead worship. This leadership style impacted me. No matter how well or kindly I was treated, I still felt out of place. Boys could read the scripture during Sunday morning service and girls could not. That was the first time I really felt that I was not on equal footing with boys—the first time I faced a "girls can't" barrier. Society wasn't the first to teach me that—the church was.

Hearing disempowering words in my teenage years turned my stomach open, swallowing every bit of who I thought I could be. It didn't help that I was a child who read the Bible on her own. I didn't have the tools to even be sure of what I knew. The Bible is complex; a copy of a copy, a translation, a collection of universal truths and principles mixed in with stories tied to ancient cultural practices and customs. Left to a person's own devices, a child could misread or misinterpret a lot. As much as the Bible comforted, it confounded. And when there's confusion, you tend to listen to those around you, those you trust. At the time I took some of the teachings of my church seriously, but it all unraveled when I became an adult.

Oppression of Black people is often rooted in Eurocentric interpretations of scripture. It's amazing how far Eurocentric ideals reach into the way Black people live their lives. When it comes to faith and lifestyle, how we think about something is influenced by what slaveholders and their supporters did during slavery—take scripture and use it to oppress. Sometimes when African Americans talk about Pan-Africanism and connecting to our ancestral lineage, there's resistance, as if this connection will kill us and do us harm. Many of us see ourselves as orphans and the "our people sold us into slavery" narrative sometimes fuels this idea. Although I can't deny the practice of slave trading in some kingdoms, I can't say for certain we know as much as we think we do. The way people latch onto what they hear without examining context or researching anything is an example of how impacted we still are by slavery.

When a warring clan invaded a village, capturing some and then selling them to Europeans, they were selling members of the group they were at war with. The practice of slavery, introduced through Islamic or Arabic influence, added a layer of complexity to the entire issue. Europeans benefited from all this infighting by being there to buy the "spoils," so to speak. Or they would kidnap people themselves. One of the most well-known cases was Senegalese princess Anta Madjiguene who was kidnapped and sold to a plantation in Cuba, then Florida. It's all much more complicated than "they sold us into slavery."

I find it odd that some Black people lean on white researchers so heavily and lean entirely on white Christian scholars to interpret scripture. There should be an expansive approach to understanding what is ancient. How do we really assess accurately? Black people have to dig, decipher and determine that for themselves. Everything has become so tainted. How many of these large, old companies that still exist today have roots in the slave trade? Banks, institutions, clothing businesses, and even the industrial revolution benefited and were often directly involved. These are all industries that Black people often support economically. There's no escaping it.

Our clothes, our shoes, our cars—all probably have ties to the slave trade. And unlike other groups, immigrant groups could in some cases could go back to their home countries, earn money, stretch the dollar and return richer. We could not. Our home, as it was known then, was no more. One of the tragedies of slavery was that European imperialist culture aimed to bind us to this land, so we may be in service to it, never to rule it. Since many of us struggled to see Africa as home, many of us made our home in Jesus—not America, but Jesus. Using this perspective, that was how Black people became Christians. Our call to Jesus came out of our suffering. We called on Jesus, and He showed up through Nat Turner, Sojourner Truth, Harriet Tubman, David Ruggles, William Still, Ida B. Wells and in every revolt (whether there were 33,250 or some other number). How this call evolved varied from person to person. Some avoided the Christian faith and chose to believe in something else or didn't believe for a myriad of reasons. For me, I knew that the God I loved was not sexist or racist and that any biblical interpretations telling me so weren't true.

Everything, especially from a different culture and time, gets translated and interpreted, and sometimes those interpretations err on the side of self-interest and not truth. I was at a time in my life when I was rediscovering true faith, not religion. What was so and what someone said was so were two different things. It made my experience working with a few white "Christian" organizations more perplexing. How some white "Christian evangelical" views merged quite seamlessly with white supremacy—like sand mixing into sand on the other side of an hourglass.

Even in my work with "Christian" entities some branded liberation theology as Marxist and certain freedoms were recast as demonic. Apparently, whom the Son sets free is not free indeed. George Washington and other enslavers, rapists and the like were rarely condemned in my presence. Maybe on TV or in a slick public relations campaign, but not so much in real life, behind closed doors, at dinner tables or in court chambers. Throughout life, there were interpretations and reinterpretations. What you believe to be true can be like a weight around your ankles holding you down, and it can take a million moments of self-reflection to break free.

My spiritual undoing—dismissing once and for all what I used to believe—and the process of redoing led to a wrestling that didn't translate into what I imagined or hoped for. It wasn't pretty, blooming, or new and soft like the flowers of my childhood. It was a quandary. I had to put the pieces together, and this was in every area of my life—social life and career. The square peg I was pressing into a round hole got stuck. I felt every aspect of my life in Colorado languishing.

My attempts to create community and build a trusted social network became a checklist of things I thought I needed to do to improve my situation—find groups through Meetup.com, go to church more often, date, teach a class, change jobs, hang out with the friends that were less in number. As it turned out, I wasn't the only one who found Colorado hard to settle into. Colorado was often a pit stop on the way to somewhere else—friends were moving away. As time passed, I grew more exhausted with my routine, and I isolated myself. At first, I thought if I left my Colorado Springs job for one in Denver, I would fare better. I would meet more people and my outlook would improve. But those opportunities didn't exist.

    I did land a volunteer position with the Aurora History Museum as a collections/archive volunteer. My role was to help preserve and catalog a memorial. One year prior, in the summer of 2012, a movie theater only three minutes from my house was shot up during a late-night screening of *The Dark Knight Rises*. I had been to that theater before but stopped going as often because I thought the seats were too dirty. Within several years of Colorado living, I'd become a bougie moviegoer. Since I was at the movies all time, I only went to the nicer theaters. I had gone to this particular theater before for a late-night movie. But tragically, on that particular night, twelve people (including one six-year-old) were murdered and seventy were injured. It was such a surreal moment—the chaos and the white male assailant gently taken into custody. Unreal. After this tragedy, a memorial made of candles, stuffed animals and notes formed outside the theater at Town Center in Aurora. It stayed there for a number of months before being moved into storage at the Aurora History Museum. Myself, along with other volunteers, inventoried each item and some items were sent to the families. Not all families responded. I can't imagine a received teddy bear, note or candle soothing unimaginable sorrow. No heartbeat, no smile, no touch, just a candle.

It was a sobering experience and an exercise in managing memory—the memorializing of tragic events. I found myself immersed in the tragedy of murder. In Philly, murder and violence were more commonplace like old wallpaper in old buildings. Philly—both a haven for enslaved Black people who'd escaped slavery and (arguably) the birthplace of modern day policing—struggled to claim complete safety. In many neighborhoods people couldn't escape violence. Now, in Colorado, I was preserving a soon-to-be artifact tied to a violent event. We wore masks as we cleaned and removed debris from candles and stuffed animals. There were so many candles, many tall Catholic candles encased in glass. Some of the notes were illegible, but I remember the children's drawings. We mostly worked in silence. I loved museums before this, but I appreciated the work more now that I was doing it. I became a participant in preserving time and all actions of human beings both tragic and triumphant.

History was a roller coaster of instances, circumstances and intentions—plots and plans, progression and regression. Museums housed the physical details of the human journey just like libraries. Proof of existence as it were. My existence in Colorado was a roller coaster slowing down. I thought about all that Colorado was—my refuge, my wide-open space, my playground, my yoga mat, my unfinished poem. I thought I could dig my fancy flats into its dry grass and red earth and settle there. But I didn't have any kids or got married or built a viable career or obtained a graduate degree or created anything, so Colorado became a check box marked tentative.

Philly was city living with more of everything. Colorado was vast. Its openness and its quiet energy were larger than

I flew in from Colorado and surprised my grandmom on her 80th birthday; she hadn't seen me in a while.

life. But Philly was eclectic with its own brand of people, food, culture, music and community. Philly pulled you in. It was small in that way. I could easily find my place there because I was a part of it. I was a native. I couldn't wrap my arms around Colorado and accept that what I had in Philly was gone. It was as if I was carrying Colorado like an oversized beach ball—my heart made contact, but my fingers never touched. I was uninspired, living in a postcard. I didn't know what to do with that. I didn't know how to make Colorado smaller.

Although Black people were small in number, one of the past mayors of Denver was a Black man, and I noticed how some professional Black men excelled more than Black women. I wondered if there were more opportunities for Black men on average, but I only knew what I happened to see. I didn't have in-depth knowledge regarding how well Black professional women were doing. Maybe the imbalance I perceived was just that, a perception. The difficult task of finding work in Denver—so I could leave Colorado Springs—remained difficult. Even though I only bothered applying for jobs I was qualified for, the search was unfruitful. I also struggled with being away from home and family. My grandmother was sick at the time and the idea of moving seemed inevitable. So one day I decided to look for book-editing positions in Philly and came across a product development position in nursing education. I applied. After two editing tests and three interviews, I was hired and just like that—I was out of Colorado, again.

## Train Travel

A scenic ride cross-country
leaves a trail of memory
Quick snapshots of endless landscape
flash and scroll through time.
Past and present ideas of home
skip ahead and trace outlines anew.
And I pass and pass and pass
to arrive back in time to present time.

## Chapter 10

# DASH

### Fleeting Health and the Corporate Escape

I didn't have a chance to prepare for my move back to Philly. A few days after putting in my two-week notice, I ended up in the hospital. It was 2013 and I was there for almost the entire month of May with a collapsed right lung that would not resolve after two chest tubes. Even though I saw top-notch doctors regularly with annual checkups, it didn't matter. Essentially, they acted as reactionary providers, waiting for a health crisis—one Yale educated and the other, Mayo Clinic trained. I still ended up in the hospital. Whenever I scheduled an appointment for pain or other symptoms, my tests came back normal—normal blood work, normal x-rays—hence, no action from the physician. They all missed my future endometriosis diagnosis and their lack of follow through and care stretched back years.

The end result was lung surgery, a pleurodesis. A rather traumatic exit to my time in Colorado, my mom flew in to be with me and took me by train all the way back to Philly. Patients who recently had lung surgery couldn't travel by air. My mom reserved two Amtrak tickets for the sleeper-car trains. The sleeper cars were outfitted with bunk beds and a shower, which stood in the middle of the small space. Opposite the shower was a modest table with two chairs pressed against a window looking out into the open. We went from Denver to Chicago, changed trains in Chicago, boarded a train to Pittsburgh and then caught the last train to Philly. The train to Chicago was most scenic. I was pretty sick and could barely walk up the stairs to our sleeper car, but the views were amazing. We met a nice older couple from Canada who took train rides frequently. They told us, "You've got to take the train from Colorado to California. It is breathtaking." Something I made note of in my head since it wasn't something I'd do anytime soon. My focus was on the problem at hand—pain.

Once in Philly, I scheduled a doctor's appointment and managed to start walking longer distances shortly after. I felt sick on and off for two years. Feeling sick became so normal I told many people I was fine even though I wasn't. Honestly, I felt bad for so long I didn't remember normal, couldn't remember healthy. I seemed to be at the doctor's office every few weeks and I was tired all the time. I stopped driving long distances. If my destination was more than 15 minutes away, I took the train. If I couldn't take the train, I stayed home. I started working within two weeks of being back in Philly.

Fortunately, in my new position, I didn't have to deal with a horrible supervisor on top of being sick. My new job brought me one of my best bosses. She was white, but I was relieved that she wasn't mean or crazy. I had no misgivings about my decision to work for this company and no complaints at first. I could heal in peace. *Could this job be my last stop before retirement? My corporate love song?* I wondered. As I settled in, I learned that the company, despite the encouraging welcome, was unstable and departments regularly went through a reorganization. Every time our bottom-line numbers were lower than projected, the company would restructure departments. I survived three of these "reorgs." Some sects of the book-publishing industry struggled. Print sales were declining, and department heads and VPs were trying to stop the bleeding, so to speak, and create new avenues for greater financial stability and increased profits. The popularity of e-books, audiobooks, and online content surged, and publishing companies decreased spending by hiring less staff and outsourcing many publishing duties, such as copyediting, to other countries outside the US. As a result, publishers were giving editors more books to work on.

    They consolidated roles; one person now performed roles that were once separated. Editorial assistants were few and so were interns. Developmental editing was outsourced as well. Editors adopted more project management duties and could be working on more than 10 books at one time (300- to 900-page books). Each book in a different stage of the process, but an overwhelming feat nonetheless. There was a time when an editor would have 2-3 books on their plates at any given time. Those were the days, but those days were long gone. I couldn't be as attentive to each author. I juggled and multi-tasked and smiled, trying to rediscover the joy of creating books. But the industry had become an unhealthy dungeon, a cesspool of unrealized creativity, exhaustion and depleted energy.

    Every day I walked up the stairs of Suburban Station and down JFK to my building—a high-rise. Up the elevators and through the key card entry doors were empty cubicles. I always arrived while it was often still dim outside. Early mornings held back the sun, and the only sound I'd hear was dripping coffee, the hum of the refrigerator and the chatter of CNN anchors, which came from the large screen TV in the break room. I could take in the view of the city from the large windows and take in the ambiance of the moment—this healing chapter in Philly, visits to see my ailing grandmother and the anticipation of something comforting on my lips—like tea. *Was this the beginning or end of a book-publishing love affair?* My co-workers would trickle in. We would complain about our jobs and talk about our weekends, our families, our futures. The crew complained and laughed over coffee and walks during lunch. We helped each other succeed.

Days moved like a seesaw. The better I performed at my job, the more work I received. I couldn't handle the workload. I was even working on the weekends at times. I was being assigned more and more books. I even worked during our annual holiday party. My boss had no control over this, and while drowning, my health was affected—it was me or this job. I weighed two choices: go on sick leave or find a less demanding position. I applied for another job as an editorial project manager at a smaller book publisher. I jumped ship. It was a difficult decision because I loved my boss. As much as I didn't want to, I moved on only to be ushered into the next phase of my book publishing experience. One often thinks nothing can be worse than what has already been endured, but that isn't at all true. It can always get worse.

This smaller textbook publisher was located in a dinky rundown building not far from my last job. The building, a striking contrast from where I worked before, should have been a sign. Previously, I worked in a high rise, complete with front entrance security and two restaurants on the main floor. A modern office, our break rooms had flat-screen TVs and a lounge with city views. There were even huddle rooms and meeting places where editors could hold private conference calls with authors. This new place had no elevator and no meeting places for author meetings. Editors were expected to hold their author meetings out in the open at their cubicles. Indeed, a fall from grace. The building had fluctuating temperatures, power outages and awkward workspaces. The supervisors were inexperienced. I literally found it hard to believe that such a poorly run company made money. But it was a company that had been around for a long time. There was this "fly by the seat of your pants" way of operating and no training for new staff (at least no training for me). Much of the workflow didn't make sense. It was like they fell ass-backwards into money.

When I arrived at this small publisher, there were no ground rules or orientation. Every job I held prior had a training process. A tour of—this person handles this task; this is how we handle permissions; some companies do this, but here we do that. When I started my new position, I would ask about specific procedures and my supervisor would address a different topic altogether, so I ended up learning from other editors. The white editors had more information and could direct me to where the files were and who typically handles what.

My boss also didn't know basic publishing terminology. So sometimes I had to explain terms to her even though *The Chicago Manual of Style* was readily available at the office. She would make up her own terms. I felt like I was constantly teaching my boss what she should already know. Because she was my boss, I let her use whatever terminology she wanted. I followed suit and used the wrong terminology so I wouldn't be viewed as combative. When someone with limited knowledge is your supervisor, you actively avoid being called a know-it-all, which is easier said than done. For a Black person to know more about a particular topic, even if insignificant, it can trigger prejudiced people. It brings out hostility, insecurity and resentment. White supremacists have delicate egos.

My job was hampered further by problems I inherited from a former employee. I replaced someone who, despite keeping poor records, worked there for years. It wasn't a complete disaster, but a part of my day would be spent researching books where records were missing. As if that wasn't enough, infighting among department heads deadlocked us, so processes were never fully agreed upon. Instead, I was forced to proceed and wait for someone to tell me I was doing something wrong, because, at the end of the day, the primary objective was to get each book out on time. As long as the book was released on time, quality and proper record keeping or proper procedures was a secondary goal. A late book automatically meant no money, and errors? Well, that's what reprint corrections are for. And when I say quality, I'm not just referring to missed grammatical mistakes, I'm referring to a missing acknowledgments page, a jacked-up index or some other content-related issue. I also mean a lack of oversight regarding issues of cultural insensitivity and/or racist content.

A prime example of this lack of oversight was discovered while working on a title that included a chapter on interacting with different ethnicities. The point of the chapter was to teach nursing students about various cultures. Its objective was to increase the cultural competency of nursing students, so they were more equipped or prepared in treating patients of diverse backgrounds. The premise or intention of the course was commendable, but the content was stereotypical and included a lot of assumptions and cultural practices taken out of context. This content had been in the book for years, and no one noticed how problematic it was. Rumors circulated that old staff, no longer with the company, were aware of the problem but didn't address it. This time, the acquisitions editor assigned to this title received feedback from a reviewer. After seeing the feedback, she asked me to take a look. I was the project manager assigned to this title.

Publishers use reviewers all the time, especially before a book goes into its next edition. Reviewers mull over the current content and comment on anything out of date or missing. This book was being updated for the 5$^{th}$ edition and it was assigned to me a few months prior. Before editors/project managers begin working on new editions, the book is reviewed and the acquisitions editor holds a meeting with the project manager and provides details regarding the results of the review, and other important information, such as pub date, schedule, budget, art and cover design. I was in her office when I first read the pages on culture.

When I read through it, I noticed right away that the material was stereotypical, inaccurate and offensive. I wasn't sure if the acquisitions editor handling this title had the cultural maturity and insight to fully understand my point of view. Corporate America is bursting at the seams with culturally ignorant professionals who often don't understand what's offensive and why. When it comes to anything racial, especially when it comes to Black culture, white staff don't often think critically, especially if they haven't studied those topics. She was no exception.

I told her the content was offensive and should come out of the book. That was my immediate response. I went into detail about why because she looked bewildered. She didn't quite understand why it was offensive, but she took my reaction to heart, and when she met with the publisher, she told him that offensive content was discovered and would be revised or taken out. Not long after that, an African American student, who went to a school that assigned this particular book, was appalled at the content and expressed her outrage on Twitter. The CEO of the company found out about it and held an emergency meeting with marketing and other executives to decide what should be done about this sudden PR nightmare. The decision was made to release an emergency reprint, removing the entire chapter from the book. I thought it was a great first step. They were taking immediate action, and a public statement was to follow.

My boss met with me and told me of the decision. I was the editor assigned to the book, so I would be preparing the manuscript for the reprint. The CEO questioned the acquisitions editors about why the content had been there for several editions. No one caught it, really read it or knew enough about Black culture to flag it. But in retrospect, it was quite a circus. As it turned out (after later research), that very same content has had complaints attached to it since 2010. There was even a legal trail. Many professors spoke out regarding specific textbooks from this company, yet executives acted like it was a new finding. I didn't truly know how common this issue was in book publishing at large, because there weren't enough Black editors around and I did not get a chance to review every book that had racial content. But that being said, I do not feel that Black editors should be pigeonholed in this way. We should be given opportunities to lead the way in all aspects of book publishing and not just in matters of race.

When it comes to racial content, many white editors either do not recognize or do not know how to address racism, which means they aren't necessarily concerned enough to solve the problem. In my last position, my boss would come to me and ask me informally about something she read and I would provide insight. But, generally speaking, there aren't enough Black editors or Black executives in book publishing to manage and guide the development of cultural content. No one really notices enough to care until bad PR outpaces profit. Executives don't take steps to hire professionals who can serve as authorities on this matter. Many companies talk about diversity in hiring and then "brown up" their staff just to give the appearance of racial progress. But when one or two Black editors are hired as staff, they do not always have executive power. Not enough African American editors hold executive positions in publishing, especially books that are responsible for educating America's children and young adults. To be honest, there isn't necessarily a shift in mindset just because a Black person is on staff.

The recruitment of Black English majors was scant. There were a few Black woman executives on the trade side of book publishing, but even fewer served in textbooks. The absence of Black men was a gaping hole. My hope was that these executives I heard about here and there over the years were being treated well and that they weren't just figureheads. There is nothing worse than working for a boss who can't stand you. If you're given no control over content and its placement in schools, hospitals and other institutions, it's that much harder to dismantle systemic racism. Racist publications are a part of the structural racism paradigm. But as I've experienced from the beginning of my publishing career, you sometimes expect something different or hope something will get better, but it can always get worse in some cases.

James Baldwin once said, "You think your pain and your heartache are unprecedented in the history of the world, but then you read." My issues with book publishing were among a collection of other screwed up moments in time—varying degrees of BS, varying degrees of horror. I kept working in book publishing even though I could have gone my own way sooner. *This isn't slavery. You don't have to enter through the back door. There isn't a Black bathroom. Move up or move on, but move forward.* That's what I did until it became obvious that I needed to forge a new path. I hoped I had been heard and that corporations were learning.

Business owners and executives should know that hiring Black editors who fight against white supremacy would fill a crater-sized hole in their content development process. These ideas begin to take shape on the collegiate level. The person who recruited me for my internship at Penn State Press sought to encourage more African Americans to consider a career in book publishing, specifically in university press publishing. But after me, a white student complained that he didn't have access to the internship because he was white. If I recall correctly, Penn State Press was told that they could not use race to advertise their internship. Book publishing was white because Black students were not exposed to the field and were even locked out of training opportunities to enter these publishing houses. It's not uncommon to see some white editors naturally support white supremacist principles when editing Black American history and culture. Black editors loyal to the quest for equality and justice and preserving the Black voice should always be in charge of Black content and how their culture is being represented.

Since the CEO felt blindsided by all this, he decided to have all content that addressed culture evaluated. I was not invited to be a part of the process, but when I found out what was happening, I inserted myself. This was the beginning of a rocky road ahead at this company, but I didn't want to send a message that told them locking Black people out of these discussions was okay. The person who was in charge of managing the review of cultural content, which included deciding what would be done with it, was a white man. He seemed rather comfortable taking on that role. Maybe he voted for Obama and watched *Eyes on the Prize* as a kid. I don't know what made him feel like he was up for the task. His false confidence helped no one. Some white professionals adopt mindsets driven by the following qualifiers: "I adopted a Black kid," or "I married a Black person," or "I have an in-law that is Black, so I can speak on race," and the ever so popular, "I have a Black friend." But being in close proximity to Black people doesn't entitle one to lead or have influence in Black spaces. This man, put in charge of this initiative to check all multicultural content, was white on white. He couldn't be any whiter.

There were meetings being held and emails circulating about which content was being reviewed. I took it upon myself to review the content and I relayed my concerns to my boss and the white man in charge. Behind the scenes though there was another issue percolating. A prominent African American journalist got hold of the story and mentioned the student who found the offensive content. I saw it on Facebook. I wondered where the announcement from the company was posted, and why I couldn't find any mention of the reprint online. The next working day I brought it to the attention of my boss and inquired about the announcement made regarding the release of a corrected reprint. I told her that when I Googled and searched online for the book on my office computer, I didn't find the reprint or any announcement regarding the content being removed. It looked like the company wasn't doing anything and I was confused. After asking the question via email, my boss pulled me into her office and gave me a one-hour lecture about my role and how it is not my job to follow up or inquire about what is happening. They are going to do as they see fit, and I'm lucky that they did anything. The company didn't have to do a thing. She was irate.

She also told me that she thought my email was "accusatory." I actually apologized and said that I wasn't aware that it sounded accusatory and I even asked her what made the email so brazen to her. She didn't say. Now I know how emails can easily convey hostility and anger even when it's unintentional, but I was very careful to keep it short, professional, and focused on merely asking the question rather than passing judgment. I became paranoid and read the email over and over. Was it the email? It could have been her on-edge guilt or maybe it was my deep brown sun-loved skin that sparked insolence. I wasn't formally disciplined over it, and my boss never brought it up again, but it was an enlightening experience.

My subconscious almost cussed me out. *You are there to perform as they see fit and that is all. This place is not a democracy. It is a job. Black people should be glad they have jobs at all, right? Do your job, shut up and don't push back.* I was tired and didn't want to bow down. I wanted my blood cool and light, not boiling. After the meeting, my supervisor dismissed me. It was the end of the day, so I left right after. It was a pointless conversation. I used to think that Black presence mattered, but it rarely matters unless white staff are poised for change. If not, you'll just end up being used as a pawn. Even if they ignored me because they didn't like me or my tone, my spirit or whatever, there were three other Black people on staff and they weren't considered authorities in all this. As I walked out of the building, I lamented how my boss reminded me of some of the white women characters I read about or saw in movies—seemingly clueless and genuine, while poised and ready to unleash their destructive energy. She was fem sharp; knives could've been hiding in her high heels.

Despite the lecture from my boss regarding that particular issue, I continued to give my opinion on how each cultural issue should be handled. Sometimes I could convince the editors who managed those titles to make changes and sometimes I wasn't. For example, the myth that Black Americans are more tolerant of pain or don't feel pain as much as other ethnic groups was removed. The belief that Black people don't feel or have a high tolerance for pain is one of those age-old medical myths that have withstood the test of time. It dates back to slavery. The irony of it all was the presence of my own pain.

I still dealt with pain years after my surgery. During my interviews, I asked about working from home once per week, which was the arrangement I had in my previous job. Although my supervisor seemed sympathetic, they were not accommodating. They agreed back then but magically forgot afterward. I didn't even fight it. Deep in my DNA, deep within its code, likely lies the memory of my family's various strategies for managing hardship. I think my family partially decided to "put up with" many things in the interest of survival. Like muscle memory, I was slow to put my fist in the air. You can't fight everything, right?

Maybe I should have worn a big smile—a smile as wide as Louis Armstrong's. Honestly, I don't know how pleasant I looked as I read those books. Some content was a series of stereotypes and fabrications mixed in with facts pulled from African American Studies or African American literary theory books. The flat-out lies ranged from large to minor. Even something simple, such as the difference between Voodoo and Hoodoo was too much for them to research (a simple Google search would have corrected that). But these so-called facts that are not critiqued, verified and researched spread rapidly in book publishing. They spread until the myth becomes truth to the general population, or in this case, the medical community. Judgments about how African American culture should be discussed shouldn't be left to people who don't know how to make these decisions. One of my friends who rode the train with me everyday gave me a "that's why you're there" word of encouragement. But discouraging voices surrounded me.

When publishing companies include cultural information, they must exercise responsibility. If qualified personnel are not on staff, those books should be outsourced to qualified freelancers, or they should recommend titles that handle these topics well. At the very least a board or consultancy should be created. During this time, the white man in charge hired an unqualified white developmental editor to review all cultural content. She was a freelancer he worked with extensively, but she had no background in reviewing cultural content. When she reviewed one of my titles, she flagged the content referencing slavery and the holocaust. She commented that the content should be removed because it "dates the book." I challenged this and the content stayed in. This was only possible because I could review her work and reverse any attempts to remove any parts of history that she simply didn't like. I'm not even sure she was clear on what her role was.

I wondered if these small victories amounted to much. The problem with being the only Black editor in the department or one of the few Black people in an entire company is that the company doesn't have to listen. I think about conversations I've had with other Black professionals in publishing. Most of them were in marketing, sales and manufacturing. Some of them had similar experiences and others didn't. I thought some of this had to do with the level of control. Marketing professionals, along with sales and manufacturing, are working on the back end with a product that has already been created. Editing is a part of content creation and approval. So there's much more freedom and support for people in a role that is focused on sales more so than content.

Since these books were for students, there was resistance to correcting anything. The "leave well enough alone" position was strong because many schools and instructors generally accepted what was in these textbooks. The outrage wasn't widespread yet. Companies weren't forced to change or understand. Their bottom lines weren't affected enough. *Were there not enough Black people dying due to a medical professional believing our pain wasn't serious? All traced back to a myth found in textbooks?* When companies really care about something, they will take the time to understand and solve the problem. But many would rather not address culture at all. Publishing companies that hire African American editors with a background in cultural research and history are capable of evaluating this information if they are allowed. If publishers refuse to hire African American editors, then universities and book retailers should only purchase books or sell books from publishers that care about accuracy and racial equity.

This is, in fact, an opportunity for Black-owned publishers and Black doctors to step in and take over this segment of textbook publishing altogether—a segment in which they may currently be locked out. When I think about major events in literary history, I'm struck by how much has been taken from Black people especially when it comes to our life stories. When Harriet Beecher Stowe wrote *Uncle Tom's Cabin* in 1852, she based much of her narrative on the story of Josiah Henson; his story was published in 1849. Isn't that plagiarism? When *Uncle Tom's Cabin* became a top seller, did any of those profits trickle down to Josiah Henson's estate then or now? *Uncle Tom's Cabin* is still being published, and in circulation. Of course, when Alex Haley was accused of plagiarism after *Roots* was released, there were consequences.

In fact, white-owned publishing houses sold and distributed liberation narratives—now in the public domain. Did these sales ever benefit the African Americans who wrote them and their descendants? In the textbook world, white control over Black content has led to the continued dissemination of offensive untruths about Black people. The result was some medical professionals being taught or led to mistreat, misunderstand and/or think poorly about Black people. Black doctors help curtail this, but there are often not enough Black doctors or nurses to go around. If students read these myths in a book or learn them in school, they often perceive that the content is correct. They trust their schooling, and their schooling has authority over them. Intervention in this area was needed as it impacted the life outcomes of Black patients. We can stop medical professionals from ignoring Black patients in pain or believing other falsehoods by getting accurate book content in the hands of medical and nursing school administrators and directors. Racism is taught and it permeates every area of life including how Black patients are treated.

These were the years where I learned my reach only goes so far. I was happy changes were made through the many editor roles I had with various book publishers. I wasn't sure what it would take to be more effective. The wonderful bosses that I did have weren't particularly high up the ladder of executive power. Would I have to become something I didn't want to become—agreeable, race neutral, silent? Could I be enthusiastic, cooperative and respectful of the white power structure? If so, I would have to learn how to navigate office politics even if that involved demeaning and or disregarding my people and myself.

I didn't want to believe that all of book publishing was like this, and maybe it isn't. The STEM, trade and Christian book worlds were definitely challenging. I didn't completely master the art of surviving and/or conquering the hostile corporate climate or make it far up the corporate ladder. Senior level was as high as I went, and quite frankly, I didn't know if I wanted to go any further. It may have required a certain level of black belt ninja coonery that I wasn't willing to learn. Fortunately, I performed well enough in my editing roles that I was able to switch jobs when my current job tanked. The desire for change became commonplace. I asked questions and challenged standards. When I got in trouble for doing so, there were always consequences—some I could see right away, some I couldn't. You don't always know what's in your HR file.

After the cultural review of this company's textbooks, my boss began micromanaging me. There were a series of incidents where I was denied time off for Martin Luther King's birthday (the company didn't recognize the holiday) or denied requested training. I felt I was in the middle of an attempt to derail my position there, and I grew weary of the corporate publishing space. I learned all I could, and I wasn't sure if staying would make a difference. I thought my knowledge could be applied in other ways. I had a better chance of making an impact from the outside rather than from the inside. As I entered my 20th year as an editor, I felt I could do more as an independent with my own platform. Could I have looked for another publishing job? Yes, but I didn't want to risk facing the same level of professional discontent and racism at a different company. The same song played over and over.

What did happen was that I got hungry. I caught the whiff of freedom and the smell of it led me further away from professional drama. Freedom smelled sweet and fresh like a field. The smell hit my tongue and tasted like peppermint at first and then floral like a rose-spiked tea. As time passed, I hungered for a better, boundless life. I outgrew the corporate experience and I didn't want to starve anymore. Like the seed in the diamanté poem I wrote when I was ten, a flower was springing up and I couldn't stay in the ground any longer.

I embarked on a new journey, a new path free of companies telling me how Black content should be handled. I no longer wanted to deal with the instability of publishing, the high workload or the interpersonal office politics. I wanted to bloom. I wanted to know what kind of flower I was—a wildflower or a rose, a sunflower or a lavender field. I knew at this point the seed life was over.

## Independence

Who doesn't want freedom?
It's a dream pressed against the bottom foot
It floats above your smile and settles beneath your laugh

Freedom is light and airy like swift winds
flying through every barrier
No one can contain it, and no one can lock it up.

Who doesn't want freedom?
Freedom stretches and pulls
and bears within it hope.

It does not bow,
for it is supreme,
and when you have it,
you can do as you please.

## Chapter 11

# REFLECTIONS

## My Publishing Journey

Philly's known for its texture—its grit, its perceived bad attitude, its heart, and its refined and rough strands of foul-mouthed, hand-clapping, soprano-soaring energy draped across a backdrop of varied experiences—some sweet and others absurd. The questions: would you like a little violence with your coffee or a bullet in your bathroom wall are more like directions to an area marked "must avoid." But anyone who embraces Philly can handle all this mixed in with the soul-touching melodies of the most iconic musicians of any generation. The brilliance of Philly history was complete with Black family high society—Tanner, Mossell, Robeson—and the Fortens. You have to take the bitter with the sweet to remember the undeniable magic of Philadelphia—the city of firsts.

Freedom is either chased or traced. It's pursued when it's violently withheld or represented in chalk traced around a murdered body. You're either bound or dead. Someone frees you through death or someone tries to keep you bound in life. The absurdity of the two perspectives is what we ought to fight against. Although freedom is a human right, those rights often need to be taken or fought for. The American institution of slavery that my mother's side and father's side endured was merely a step in the direction of true freedom. Freedom is like a multi-sided puzzle with layers of complexity—jumbled Rubik's Cubes stacked on top of each other. One side is red, and the other side is a jumbled mix of everything from colorism to all forms of race-based discrimination. Every step toward freedom reveals another mess to undo. What does freedom even look like?

There are more African American women in book publishing today than in 1998 when I first started, but the industry is still very white. Every few years or so, I'd read an article that mentions the lack of diversity in publishing. It always made me smirk. Acknowledging that publishing companies don't prioritize diversity is like saying, "In today's news, please know that water is still wet, thank you." Those articles never really got to the heart of the matter, which is that many publishers don't welcome Black editors and Black college students aren't encouraged to enter the book editing/production field. I'd never even met a Black book layout designer. Since there are so few Black-owned book publishers hiring staff, the opportunities are typically with white presses. Plus, the search for acceptance and value in a majority-white publishing company can be exhausting. It's like trying to push an elephant off of a ledge. Proving oneself doesn't necessarily spark genuine change.

Change begins when companies agree something is wrong. When there is change, the process of transformation or elimination begins. When any system is considered detrimental, society will eliminate the problem or force it to become something else. We see this with the growth of the renewable energy industry. When people noticed that pollution and the burning of fossil fuels were damaging, new ways of energy production and waste management developed. Essentially, it's all a part of progress and humankind's journey forward. My own journey led me to Colorado where I came to understand life outside of a predominately Black artistic context. It came on the heels of my literary journey, which started when I was a child—a shy, anxious, hidden child dreaming about my future life.

In corporate America, freedom was a bit of a pipedream. There were times I could stretch my creative muscles, and there were times when the air wore tights and pranced around in bold entitlement, limiting Black influence. I enjoyed the most freedom working outside of book publishing in quality assurance. Corporate America, which was probably true for many industries, thrives on the principles of conformity and assimilation. Yes, one can be creative, but the employee was given objectives and goals. The employee was not creating in a vacuum. The employee does not own anything. Employees were part of a team, a collective, and to ensure professional survival, one was implored to go with the flow. The desire to collaborate and set the rules wasn't always realized. After many years, I decided that I did not want to follow, and I didn't want a company telling me how I should express my Blackness or evaluate Black issues or navigate American work culture and life.

The very idea of working as an independent was a huge confidence booster. I realized I knew more than I thought. When people would ask me questions about publishing or ask me for advice, I actually knew what I was talking about. I wasn't incompetent. Corporate America can shatter a person's confidence. Sometimes you feel that everyone else is so much better than you, even though sometimes the work from those very same people is mediocre at best.

When I planned my exit from the corporate book world, I imagined my life as an independent—the freedom, the open doors. I get to refocus my attention and redefine what the real work should be. I could reshape and redirect my publishing experience and editing skills to align with new objectives that would forge a new path. An editor who thinks beyond literary standards and books and stretches forward to help transform racist societies—bringing more light, depth and knowledge into the world. I did not want to contribute to present-day complacency.

Over the course of hundreds of years, Black people have battled the suppression and oppression of Black thought, ideas and the implementation of those ideas. Instead of widespread progress for all, we have handfuls of wealthy Black people achieving that wealth through narrow entrepreneurial pathways that do not translate into generational wealth on a grander scale. Some get through, but not all get through because this window of opportunity is small and narrow for Black people. Structural racism, which first began through white terrorism, was expressed through the burning down of wealthy communities and Black businesses.

How would publishing fit into all this? Books and the passing down of stories and information helped push the abolitionist movement, and it can push us forward today. Books, textbooks and guides forge a path toward institutional restructuring and influence. They hold a legacy, an account, a genetic record like DNA. Publishing infiltrates any and everything under the sun. A major problem today is that many books that can help spur change are buried in libraries and not taught in schools or used in training facilities. We lack access and control, some of which can be gained through voting, thereby increasing political power—states often control curriculum.

Helping the Black community use publishing to spearhead change and not just spark conversation is a worthwhile path.

America's constant desire to converse without implementing solutions has left the Black community on an endless climb. They end up being conversations that just repeat over and over again over decades. Although these conversations are never-ending, we can't afford for change to stop. Black people are too tired to deal with more rounds of lip service. Publishing is one of many avenues that can dismantle racist systems.

We need to set ourselves free from it all, which is a daily process. Freedom is a process. When I think about each position I held in book publishing, they all cooperate to reach a singular goal and that is to meet the educational needs of the audience and/or the institution. Books are influential over mindsets and ideologies and behaviors; it impacts reason. As media informs, sparks movements and supports change, books infiltrate systems of learning in ways that are much deeper. Books, as well as pamphlets, are integral to every system of education. Racists are taught, freedom fighters are taught. If we can impact education, we can create our own allies. We don't have to convince or hope an enemy becomes cooperative or catches the vision. It's very hard to move people who already have their minds made up; their minds have already been shaped.

Allies in the Black community come and go. Knowing who's an ally is like playing a round of poker. You don't know what hand people are playing with until they lay their cards down. Symbolic gestures of unity are appealing but have often left us with not much to show for it decades later. The continued despair has led to more violence in Black communities, more Black men and women jailed, an unchanging wealth gap (even with college education added to the mix) and less civic engagement. But that doesn't tell the entire story either. We are not where we used to be and many Black families have achieved levels of happiness and achievement, but we cannot stop there. Almost every Black movement has had allies, but we lose them when we try to move toward transforming Black communities and positioning them on equal footing with other groups. Dr. Martin Luther King, Jr. lost many supporters after he moved toward economic empowerment. For progress to continue, we need to be more intentional about addressing systems of oppression.

When groups are trying to change mindsets and achieve loyalty, they do so using media for immediate impact. When groups want to bring deeper longstanding change, they use books, whether that's the Bible, the Art of War, the Koran, Mein Kampf, medical textbooks or other texts. The goal is to teach, not individuals, but large groups and populations. The book publishing industry has been front and center on this front. Black publishers can be a part of this process. Whether or not this can be done from inside white publishers is unknown to me. Based on my own narrow experience, white editors can work their way up the corporate ladder and become directors, VPs, board members and presidents/CEOs. They can gain access to powerful positions sometimes regardless of degree or background.

This is especially true for white women. Unfortunately, white supremacy often trumps the assumed female camaraderie and upliftment found in feminism. Feminism and affirmative action have greatly improved the corporate success of white women. Black women have not benefited as greatly from white women's upward mobility in book publishing. White women hold most of the leadership positions, while white men are sometimes the holders of the purse strings. They are presidents, owners or on a board of directors. In a nutshell, they oversee but men didn't necessarily get too involved in day-to-day affairs. I rarely saw Black men in the book publishing space as editors.

## REFLECTIONS

I knew of one Black man who worked in the permissions department at a major Big Five publisher in New York. He told me that in the seven years he worked there, he was never promoted despite performing his job well. There was no path for him. They purposefully kept him in the same role. He ultimately left that company. But that was the only Black man I knew who held a corporate publishing job. I think the exclusive unwelcoming nature of some book publishers keeps Black people out even when they are familiar with book editing as a career path. Why consider a career in book publishing when it's so much more satisfying to write, self-publish or create your own magazine and be the editor-in-chief of that? Corporate racism is stressful and exhausting.

I never asked Black male writers why book editing wasn't a career goal. But honestly, I didn't know many well enough to ask. Why break a door down when it's much more fulfilling to forge ahead as an independent? When you compare the two, freedom is always better. As a Black woman editor, I was not always seen as a part of the team but rather a part of the company's administrative support. I was almost always the only Black person on staff, so it was pretty easy for anyone to be dismissive or not value my presence. I was often under more scrutiny because not many Black editors had gone before me, so I had to prove that I belonged there—all the time.

While a much larger pool of diversity and support often surrounded African American journalists, the corporate book publishing space offered little support. I had to look for ways to advance my learning, seek out training, ask questions, and learn to problem solve as issues arose. I did not have access to Black mentors, and honestly, I didn't know enough about mentoring to seek it out. Even though book publishing was at times an unwelcoming space, I wanted to learn the industry. My desire to learn was greater than my desire to be comfortable. As I desired more responsibility and power, I faced the repeated reality.

I had to build up a tolerance for microaggressions and blatant prejudice. Sometimes I was good at this and other times I wasn't. I quickly learned that fighters don't go far. Wherever I worked, internal opportunities for upward mobility were rare anyway. Many editors stayed in roles for 10-plus years, and VP or executive editor positions didn't often open up, and when they did, white editors filled those roles. My strategy for moving up in the ranks was simply moving on to a different company. It proved to be a good strategy, which led to great exposure. What's amazing about job-hopping is that I saw how various companies approached workflow, procedures, promotions, job duties and company restructuring. I observed what gets outsourced and to whom, how freelancers were managed, and who earned more money and why. It was an up-close review of how publishing companies handled revenue loss and their processes for implementing solutions. I had a front-row seat to witness successes and failures.

Each industry in book publishing has its own process, position titles, procedures, workflow and chain of command, but generally, the duties are the same—acquire, edit, design, print, market and sell. But how a publisher chooses to get from acquisition to bound book varies. All publishers have acquisitions editors and development editors (either in-house or freelance). Copy editors and proofreaders are also either in-house or freelance, while art and design handle custom interior layout design, cover design, illustration design, and art resizing and editing. Manufacturing/printing manages paper selection, cover materials and the binding process. They also handle reprint corrections (corrections made after a book is printed, which are completed before the next print run or immediately if it's an e-book). Then there are editorial project managers that manage the authors, the schedule/deadlines, permissions, peer review, the editorial budget, the developmental editing process and the production process to ensure that books are published on time. They often control the entire publishing process and may even perform some copyediting and proofreading themselves. Last, of course, is marketing and sales—comp copies, book expos and strategy sessions with sales reps.

As an editor, I moved back and forth between editing and project management. I observed and practiced in various editor roles. Those who focused on acquiring manuscripts, those who focused on developing manuscripts, those who focused on correcting grammar, those who participated in the final stages of proofreading, those in leadership and those who performed project management. Editors served in acquisitions, editorial or production. In publishing houses, I mainly worked in editorial and production as a content developer, project manager, copy editor and proofreader.

Editorial is where content is developed, and production is where content is refined, polished and sent to the printer. Although I always desired to work in acquisitions, I was never groomed or offered an opportunity in that area. There was an air of superiority and entitlement when it came to those roles. Acquisitions editors were the face of the company. They traveled to conferences and met with authors at expensive venues. They courted authors they thought could bring publishing companies huge profits. One can also look at the acquisitions role as a type of PR position; they were rarely Black.

As a worker bee, I was recognized for my hard work and meeting deadlines, but there was little opportunity to advance. When I performed well as an editor, my reward was that I got to keep my job. That usually meant I got more work, not more benefits. The opportunities for training and advancement always went to white editors because they were being groomed for higher-level positions. The Black editors I knew of were usually kept in the same roles all the time. The industries that were more welcoming and progressive were in quality assurance. These were rewarding but non-creative roles. The corporate publishing world can be quite restricting. It felt like a grape being crushed in a wine press. I wanted to set myself free, to drink the sweet wine of freedom.

There's also the relationship between Black editors and white editors. It's two-sided like sandpaper—one side smooth, the other rough. I expected more camaraderie and collaboration between Black and white women in the corporate world, but instead, I found myself on one side or the other of these sandpaper relations. I could never tell when I would have a smooth experience or a rough one, whether the white women I worked with were allies or untrustworthy enemies. Although book publishing was dominated by girl power, there was more backbiting than sisterhood even within groups of white editors.

One highlight was that many of my working relationships with white co-workers were fun-filled and solid like hard candy with soft centers. I could count on many of my co-workers to be easy to work with and awesome team players, but relationships with my supervisors were often filled with strife. Not often do people discuss the unspoken power struggle between white women and Black women. Both groups have faced oppression in some form. White women enjoyed privilege and benefited from the socio-economic construct of white supremacy, and some opposed the confines of white male patriarchy. But even with those trials, their future is more secure whether under a man or not. White women bear the weight of sexism, but not racism and not colorism.

## REFLECTIONS

Working for myself or in a different climate afforded me the opportunity to interact with people of all races without the complication of supervisor/employee dynamics. I don't have to feel pressured, controlled or unwelcome. I chose my clients and partners. When choosing, there's less discomfort, uneasiness or disrespect. In this position, I would be able to move forward using publishing as an avenue of change without the usual hindrances. It's the repositioning that made a difference. I was in a position of power. Independence was empowering. It greatly impacted my mental health. I didn't have to tolerate toxic behavior. I could set my own hours and be selective about who I wanted to work for. No horrible bosses. I could take better care of myself.

My experience in Colorado as a Philly native provided a great perspective. Living in opposites allows you to see the full range of how various groups of people live, interact with each other and adapt. What would have happened if I had never left Philly? Maybe I'd be married with kids or working the same job for 20 years. Colorado was representative of my freedom to choose something different. I saw things I could never have seen. I hiked and went white water rafting. I took long drives and formed bonds with people from other regions of the country. I developed a new sense of knowing due to living in unknown territory. All that I had learned would prepare me for the future, a future still being written. Life can be more of the same thing over and over again or it can be a winding path leading to something better. Now, I'm in a garden. I'm enjoying the sun. My spirit is lifted high off the ground. I fly up, up, up and high, and higher toward the sky, bending low to the soil, and whichever way it blows. I'm now riding freedom's wave as long as God carries me.